Strugglers

When Wendy has an epileptic fit in the kitchen and burns herself, her friends in their last term at a special school come up with a way to help. They set themselves a goal and spend their last days struggling to reach it.

A witty, energetic and remarkable piece of young people's theatre, **Strugglers** won the Sunday Times Playwriting Award in 1988 at the National Student Drama Festival and was revived at the Battersea Arts Centre later the same year.

Richard Cameron was born in Doncaster, South Yorkshire. A teacher for many years, he was Director of Scunthorpe Youth Theatre from 1979 to 1988 and Head of Drama at the Thomas Sumpter School in Scunthorpe until summer 1991, when he gave up teaching in order to devote himself to writing full-time. His plays include **Haunted Sunflowers**, now retitled **Handle with Care**, (National Student Drama Festival and Edinburgh Fringe Festival, 1985) which won the 1985 Sunday Times Playwriting Award; **Strugglers** (Battersea Arts Centre, 1988), which won the 1988 Sunday Times Playwriting Award; **The Moon's the Madonna** (National Student Drama Festival, Edinburgh Fringe Festival and Battersea Arts Centre, 1989), which was shortlisted for the Independent Theatre Award and won the 1989 Company Award at the NSDF and **Can't Stand Up for Falling Down** (Edinburgh Fringe Festival and Hampstead Theatre, London, 1990) for which he won the Sunday Times Playwriting Award for a record third time in 1990, as well as a Scotsman Fringe First and the 1990 Independent Theatre Award. The latter two plays are also published by Methuen.

Strugglers

A Play by
Richard Cameron

Methuen Drama

Methuen Young Drama

First published in Great Britain in 1991 by Methuen Drama,
Michelin House, 81 Fulham Road, London SW3 6RB and
distributed in the United States of America by HEB Inc, 361
Hanover Street, Portsmouth, New Hampshire, NH 03801
3959.

ISBN 0-413-65690-X

A CIP catalogue record for this book is available from the
British Library.

The photograph on the front cover is by Allan Tittmus,
copyright © Times Newspapers Ltd.

Printed and bound in Great Britain
by Cox & Wyman Ltd, Cardiff Road, Reading

Introduction

The idea for the play came out of taking a group of fourth and fifth year students from the comprehensive school where I work to a special school. They were to devise and carry out a variety of learning activities through drama for youngsters of the same age with learning difficulties. The project involved us in the school for a week. I'm not sure if my lot taught them anything, but it was a great success in terms of what they taught us about friendship, about trust, and about . . . well, about how to be happy. The overriding impression of that week in a special school was that it was full of happy, helpful people.

I began working on the play through a series of workshops with a group of my students. First of all they created the characters for me – Victor, Hannah and Billy came fairly quickly, and their strength seemed to help the others 'find' their characters. I began to write scenes for them, and to try out various situations to put them in – in launderettes, shops, discos – and at the end of about six weeks we had some rock-solid characters that could make a scene work in whatever situation I put them.

The story became one of a group about to leave the school. It was this slipping away, letting go of the safety and security of the school, into the often cruel reality of life outside, that for us gave the play a sadness which overlaid all the humour. Growing up and getting on out there is difficult enough for most of us – it's a hell of a lot more difficult for the Victors and Hannahs of this world.

In production I suggest you experiment and try out different improvisations, just to get to know the characters better. Take them shopping – not in your acting space, I mean *really* take them shopping. Get Victor and Billy in Asda, or take the lot of them to a park for the afternoon and watch what happens. As well as being good fun, it helps to build up trust between you, makes what you've got stronger, and helps create a real ensemble piece of work. I suggest you keep set and props to an absolute minimum, or it will all get in the way of what should be fast and fluid scene changes. In the original production a gym bench was used for the classroom scenes – you don't need desks and chairs to create a classroom. House scenes were simply specifically lit areas – some on the flat, some on rostra. The teacher needs to be fixed in your vision somewhere in the centre of the audience. The careers interviews can be done on a stool permanently placed right up against the audience, with teacher close, facing you.

Richard Cameron
April 1991

Strugglers was first performed at the National Student Drama Festival in 1988, and then at the Battersea Arts Centre, London, later the same year.

Characters

Pupils at St Peter's Special School:

Victor, *16, a friendly, loving boy, easily upset by all the sorrows in the world.*

Bernard, *16, likes sport, has to be busy.* **Hannah**'s *boyfriend. Physically mature.*

Billy, *16, tiny. Always on the move. Inventive imagination.*

Rufus, *16, very shy, awkward. No self-confidence.*

Hannah, *16, hearing and speech difficulties. Shy, loving, sensitive.*

Lyndsay, *16, loving, friendly, happy.*

Janet, *16, loud, a little crude, but very loving.*

Wendy, *16, quiet, withdrawn.*

Darrell, *18,* **Hannah**'s *brother. Unemployed.*

Linda, *18,* **Billy**'s *sister. Hairdresser.*

Jane, *13–14,* **Rufus**'s *cousin.*

Young Woman, *17–19, who is 'living with' a man and has his child.*

Art Lesson

Hannah, Bernard, Rufus, Victor, Billy, Lyndsay, *and* **Janet** *are drawing and painting.*

Janet What's that?

Billy A pig.

Janet Miss, he's drawing a pig and there isn't a pig. (*Gets up, comes forward.*) Miss, he's drawing a pig and there isn't one.

Billy Yes there is.

Janet Where, then?

Billy (*pointing at her*) There, then.

Janet You've had it.

Lyndsay Fight, fight!

Billy (*dodging*) Fat cow.

Janet You're going to get smacked. (*Stops suddenly.*) Miss, he's calling me names. Miss I'm only – Yes, Miss. (*Sits down again.*)

Billy *reluctantly gets up, comes forward.*

Billy Miss, I'm sorry. Miss, I'm supposed to look after the gerbil in Mr Tong's room but she took it off me and it bit her finger so she chucked it back in the cage and sat on it and bent it.

Victor *has come forward to show his picture*

Victor I've finished my picture. It's an alien from another planet, Miss. From Mars. It's a marshmallow from Mars. Miss, guess why I'm an alien? 'Cos my mum says I'm on another planet half the time. (*Laughs.*)

Victor *moves back to his seat, making alien noises. All start packing away except* **Hannah.**

Lyndsay We've got to pack away it's nearly bell time.

Hannah Oh, all right. Thank you. (*Looks up to teacher.*) No, Miss. (*Holds down her picture.*)

Lyndsay Miss, she won't show you.

Hannah It's not very good, Miss.

Lyndsay It is, Miss, it's ace. Go on, show her.

Some of the others gather round for a look – 'Let's have a look' etc. **Hannah** *tries to hide it but* **Janet** *and* **Lyndsay** *are pushing her out to the front.*

Janet It's a love picture.

Hannah No it's not.

Janet I saw it. It's a man and woman kissing under a banana tree.

Hannah No.

Janet Yes it is, then. I've seen it before, anyway. She's copied it.

Hannah I haven't copied it.

Janet You have. I've got it in a magazine.

Hannah Don't, Janet.

Janet (*mimicking*) 'Don't Janet'.

Hannah *suddenly rips up the picture. 'Oooohs' from the group. The pieces are put in the bin.*

Janet (*to teacher*) I'm not teasing her, Miss.

Lyndsay Miss, is it my turn for my careers interview after break? It's supposed to be Wendy's turn but she's away. (*Pause.*) Oh, good. (*To* **Janet**.) What do I miss?

A bell goes and they begin filing out. **Rufus** *stays to tidy up,* *clearing away pots, etc.* **Bernard** *retrieves* **Hannah***'s torn picture from the bin and puts it in his pocket. Looks to teacher.*

Bernard What, Miss? (*Comes forward.*) I haven't got a black eye. Yeah, well I had a fight with this kid, Miss, last night. (*Pause.*) No, Miss, I won. He just caught me when I weren't ready.

He goes. **Rufus** *potters about. Someone calls to him from outside and we can hear other playground noises.*

Rufus (*coming to front*) Have you got any more jobs you want doing, Miss?

Disappointed, he goes out.

The Playground

Billy (*to* **Victor**) Your great-grandad isn't anybody.

Victor He's dead, isn't he?

Billy He never was anybody.

Victor Yes he was, then. I'm telling you he was Victor Sylvester and I'm called after him.

Billy Your name isn't Sylvester.

Victor It doesn't have to be. Anyway, that's why I'm called Victor.

Billy I've never heard of him. What did he do?

Victor I've told you, he had a band. Victor Sylvester's Ballroom Dance Band and he had lots of ballrooms named after him all over England.

Billy Yeah, I bet.

Victor We've got a family tree!

Billy Yeah, it grows nuts on it!

Billy *runs off,* **Victor** *chasing.* **Bernard** *comes over to* **Hannah** *and gives her the torn picture.*

Hannah Thank you, Bernard.

Bernard I'll nick you some sellotape next lesson.

Hannah No.

Bernard *wanders off.* **Janet** *and* **Lyndsay** *come over.*

Janet What did he say?

Hannah I wish you hadn't told him I fancy him.

Lyndsay I never told him you fancied him.

Janet You did, you liar.

Lyndsay I know, but he didn't say he thought you were crap.

Janet He never said anything when we told him, did he, Lyndsay?

Lyndsay No.

Janet He could have said tell her she's ugly.

Lyndsay Yeah. But he never said anything so that means he must like you.

Janet Or be in love with you. Bernard's in love with Hannah.

Hannah Don't say any more to him, please. Promise.

Bell goes. They disperse. **Lyndsay** *brings a chair forward.*

Lyndsay's *Careers Interview*

Lyndsay (*reading from a sheet*) Lyndsay Duncan, 21
Bentinct Street. Mother – (*Looks up.*) Miss, she doesn't
work there now, she works at Kwiksave on the tills.

My career ideas: dancer, singer, shoe shop assistant.

(*Looking up.*) I don't want to do that any more, Miss. I
only put that because of my mum working in a shoe shop
and I thought she might be able to get me a job. But she
left.

(*Reading.*) My work experience. I worked at Freeman,
Hardy and Willis from December 7th to 14th, last year.
Supervisor, Mrs Duncan. (*Looking up.*) Miss, she gave me
a good reference, didn't she?

(*Reading.*) Personal likes – I like dancing, going for walks,
watching TV. (*Pause.*) I'm not bothered what kind of a job
I do. I could work anywhere where you meet people and
you can have a bit of a laugh. I wouldn't mind a factory. I
don't want a lot of money because it makes you snobby,
just enough to buy some clothes and go to dances with my
mates. I know I couldn't do some jobs because you need
brains and Mrs Clark told me I wouldn't be able to do
some jobs because I'm too clumsy. I sometimes can't hold
things proper. Nursing I can't do because she said I
wouldn't be able to give injections. (*Pause.*) I'd like to be a
famous pop-singer. Like Madonna.

A bell goes.

Home Time

All are leaving class, saying their goodbyes, etc.

Lyndsay Hannah! Tell Wendy when you see her tonight that she can come to my party next week.

Hannah Yes, I will.

All are gone, except **Rufus**, *who comes to the front.*

Rufus Do you want any jobs doing, Miss? (*Pause.*) I don't mind. With my mum in hospital I'm staying at my cousin's house and I have to go past the proper school to get there. I don't want to go until they've all gone home because some of them say things and that. (*Pause.*) About going to a school for dumbos. (*Pause.*) Thanks, Miss. (*Collects some things, takes them out.*)

On the Way Home

Victor *enters, counting his steps quietly to himself.*

Victor 118, 119, 120, 121, 122, 123 . . .

Voice 1 Hey, Victor!

(**Victor** *tries to keep counting.*)

Hey, Victor!

Victor What?

Voice 1 What you doing?

Victor Going home.

Voice 2 What are you talking to yourself for?

Victor I don't know.

Voice 1 Come here. Come over here a minute. I want you.

Victor *comes to the front. The 'Voices' are either side of him.*

What do you reckon to her over there? (*Pause.*) Come on, I'm only asking your opinion. Do you reckon she goes?

Voice 2 Don't you like girls?

Voice 1 You like girls, don't you?

Voice 2 You got any fags?

Victor I don't smoke. It's bad for you.

Voice 1 You got any sweets?

Victor Yes.

Voice 1 What sweets you got?

Victor *mimes taking out sweets. Giving them away. They take the lot.*

Good lad. You're a good lad.

Pause. **Victor** *moves off, resuming his counting.*

Billy *'s House*

Billy *is watching television, copying the sounds.* **Linda** *comes over to him.*

Linda Will you be all right? Billy? Billy!

Billy What?

Linda Will you be all right?

Billy When?

Linda When I go out. (*Repeating herself.*) John's coming at seven and Mum won't be home from work till about quarter to eight.

Billy Where are you going?

Linda You sure you'll be all right?

Billy What's on telly?

Linda Promise me you'll stay in here and watch telly. Don't go upstairs, don't go in the kitchen. I'll leave you a drink and some crisps in here. Don't go getting anything out.

Billy You're supposed to be stopping here.

Linda I'm going out.

Billy My mum doesn't like you going out.

Linda I'm working all week. I need to go out. I can't stop with you all the time like I used to. I can't help it if my hours and Mum's don't fit. Don't make it awkward for me.

Billy Hey, Linda.

Linda What?

Billy Was our dad ever famous for anything?

Victor's *House*

Victor Our Father, who art in heaven, why can't everybody be nice to each other? Them boys were being a bit nasty, weren't they? I'm sorry I swore but at least I never said it out loud, only in my head. You can still hear it, though, can't you? I don't know why I get swearwords in my head. They just seem to get inside. I'm sorry. And I'm sorry about lying as well but when Billy told me about his sister meeting somebody famous off television I just started telling him about Victor Sylvester. I remember my granddad telling me about him.

Rufus *and his cousin appear. They are playing a board game.*

Victor Can I say a prayer for Rufus's mum? She is in hospital. Rufus hasn't told me what's the matter because he doesn't say much but I think she is having a baby but with her being old they keep them in hospital, don't they? He says he likes being with his cousin. She got the 'Game of Life' for Christmas and they play it a lot, he said. I suppose it's good practice for when we all leave school.

Janet *and* **Lyndsay** *appear, in* **Janet**'s *house.*

I'm getting a bit worried about leaving now it's getting so near. I hope you'll keep looking after all my friends once we've all left. Even though we won't see each other much I know you'll make sure we're all still thinking about each other. I know it depends on the Prime Minister and not you, but will you try to get us jobs we like doing and meet nice people not nasty like those boys. (*Pause.*) Hang on, I think I can hear my mum calling me. I'll be back in a minute. (*Goes off.*)

Janet (*on CB radio*) Breaker Breaker 19. This is Dolly, come on back. Anybody out there got their ears on? Blue Boy? Is that Blue Boy? Hiya. It's me, Dolly. Yeah, I'm all right.

Lyndsay Let me have a go. What can I be called? Hello Blue Boy this is Madonna, do you copy? You what?

They giggle and continue to communicate with a crackling, faint 'Blue Boy'. **Victor** *returns.*

Victor It's me again. Sorry about that. She wanted me to open the sauce bottle. She's got a dead weak grip. She says she gets it from wringing out all them wet clothes. We only got a proper spinner last month.

Wendy *and* **Hannah** *appear, in* **Wendy***'s house.* **Hannah** *is combing* **Wendy***'s hair.*

I've saved my most important prayer till last. We found out today from Hannah why Wendy is off school again. She had another apple-epic fit only she had it in the kitchen and knocked a pan of boiling water and a boiled egg on top of her. I hope you can make her feel a bit better.

Wendy *looks at* **Hannah***'s picture.*

Hannah Guess who the boy is? Who do you think it is? (*Pause.*) Bernard.

Me and Bernard. (*They laugh together.*)

Corridor outside A Classroom.

Janet *and* **Lyndsay** *are fussing over* **Hannah**.

Janet What did he say?

Lyndsay Has he asked you for a date?

Janet Tell us.

Lyndsay He has, hasn't he?

Hannah *nods. The girls gasp and laugh and hug* **Hannah**.

Janet When are you seeing him?

Lyndsay What did he say?

Janet Oh, Hannah, that's brilliant.

Lyndsay Well done. Oh!

The three of them are nearly in tears. They break off and enter.

Bernard Now. Will you be my girlfriend?

Hannah Yes.

Bernard Starting now?

Hannah If you like.

Bernard *checks his watch.*

Bernard Hang on. (*Waits for second hand to reach the top.*) Go. Right, then, where are we off to tonight?

Hannah I can't tonight. I'm seeing Wendy. I promised. Anyway, we're on holiday all next week so we can see each other when we like.

Bernard Oh, yeah, half term.

English Lesson

Lyndsay *is arguing with* **Janet**.

Lyndsay No, she's coming.

Janet Well I'm not coming if she's coming.

Lyndsay Just because she's mates with Pat Wilson.

Janet They're snobs, them lot.

Their argument is suddenly stopped.

Lyndsay Miss? I was just asking her what today's date was. (*Looks at her paper.*) Three lines, Miss. (*She tries to hide her notebook.*) Miss, I was just writting down ideas in my rough book for my story. (*She brings out the book. Shows it.*) It's a list of people I'm inviting to my party. Next Thursday, Miss. Why, do you want me to put your name down? Sorry, Miss.

ers

to her seat. **Hannah** *puts up her hand.*

iss, can I go now, it's nearly quarter past?

Hannah's *Careers Interview.*

Hannah *comes forward with chair.*

Hannah (*reading*) Hannah O'Brien, 6 Westerby Court. Brother – Darrell, unemployed. Father – Miss, he doesn't live with us any more, but I think he's a driver.

My career ideas – Factory work. Animals. Artist.

(*Looking up.*) I don't really want a job with people because of not hearing and speaking properly. I would get embarrassed and customers might get annoyed if they couldn't understand what I was saying and I couldn't hear them properly. I'm too slow.

(*Reading.*) My work experience – I worked at Kwiksave from 7th to 14th December, last year. Personal manager Mr Kitchin.

(*Looks up.*) I was stacking things on shelves. One day I helped put the prices on the crisps and one day I was on collecting the trolleys up from the car park but I wasn't very good at that because I could only push a few at a time. (*Pause.*) Yes, Miss, I enjoyed working there. They were friendly to me and patient.

(*Reading.*) RAF talk.

Personal likes – I like drawing, reading, animals. Yes, Miss. Goodnight. Have a nice holiday, Miss.

Home Time

Lyndsay *is giving out invitations to* **Victor** *and* **Billy**. *She sees* **Hannah** *who is holding hands with* **Bernard**.

Lyndsay Hannah! (*She hands out invitations.*) Hannah, Bernard.

Hannah Thank you.

Lyndsay And one for Wendy.

Hannah I don't think she will be able to come. How many have you asked?

Lyndsay Fourteen, but they're not all coming.

Hannah What's wrong?

Lyndsay Janet's not my friend now.

Billy (*to* **Lyndsay**) What's RSVP?

Hannah Why not?

Lyndsay She didn't want me to invite Maxine.

Bernard (*to* **Billy**) Reply Soon Very Prompt.

Hannah It's your party.

Billy I'm coming.

Lyndsay I don't think Janet's going to come.

Hannah She will, won't she, Bernard?

Victor I'm coming too. Thank you very much for inviting me, Lyndsay.

Hannah Won't she, Bernard?

Bernard I don't know, do I? I've got my paper round. If you two are going to stand around all night like gossiping old women, I'm going.

Hannah (*to* **Lyndsay**) See you.

Bernard *and* **Hannah** *walk off, hand in hand.*

On the Way Home

Voice 1 Hey, Lyndsay! Hey, Lyndsay, aren't you talking tonight?

Lyndsay No.

Voice 2 Give us a kiss.

Lyndsay No. (*Pause.*) You can on my birthday.

Voice 2 When's that?

Lyndsay Next Thursday. I'm sixteen.

Voice 1 Are you having a party?

Lyndsay Yes.

Voice 1 Can we come?

Lyndsay I'll ask my mum.

She goes off.

Victor's House

Billy *knocks at the door.* **Victor** *answers it, eating a jam sandwich.*

Victor I'm still having my tea.

Billy I'll wait. I can be having a look through your family tree.

Victor Eh?

Billy Your family tree.

Victor (*worried*) Oh, you'd better come in. (*Shouting off.*) Mam, it's Billy. (*To* **Billy**.) It might take a long time to find it. It might be in the attic. You wait in here. (*He shoves* **Billy** *in a room and goes off.*)

A Street

Janet *enters.*

Voice 3 Hey, Janet!

Janet Bog off!

Voice 4 Hey Janet, you spas. You mongol.

Janet Go and play on the motorway, shithead.

She makes a rude sign, without stopping, and carries on her way.

Hannah's *House*

Hannah *and* **Bernard** *arrive at the house.*

Hannah Thanks for bringing me home.

Bernard That's all right.

Hannah Do you want to meet my brother Darrell?

Bernard I'd better go. See you tomorrow.

Hannah Park. Two o'clock. 'Bye.

He goes. She goes inside. **Darrell** *is playing a Casio synthesiser.*

Darrell What do you reckon to this?

Hannah Where did you get it?

Darrell Borrowed it off a mate. Listen.

He plays a riff. Not very well.

I've been practising that all afternoon.

Hannah What's it from?

Darrell I made it up.

Hannah What do you want for your tea?

Darrell Anything. I'm starving.

She goes off.

Victor's *House*

Victor If I tell him I haven't got a family tree, he'll laugh and maybe won't want to be my friend any more. I'll have to lie. I know it's bad. Can't I tell him we've sent it off? To London? Please don't let him ask my mum anything about it.

Rushes off. Stops. Comes back.

I forgot. Thank you for getting Bernard and Hannah together.

Goes.

Rufus's *Cousin's House*

Jane I found something in your bedroom.

Rufus What?

She brings out a sock puppet.

Oh.

Jane What have you got this for?

Rufus It's a puppet. Look.

Puts his hand in puppet.

Jane Make it say something.

Rufus (*as puppet*) Hello. What's your name?

Jane My name's Jane.

Rufus (*as puppet*) Hello Jane.

Jane What's your name?

Rufus (*as puppet*) Harold.

Jane It's good isn't it.

Rufus It's easy to make.

Jane Can you make me one?

Rufus If you like. It's only a sock.

Jane *takes off her sock, puts it on her hand.*

Jane (*as puppet*) Hello, Harold, my name's . . . what?

Rufus I don't know.

Jane Sue.

Rufus (*as Harold*) Hello, Sue.

Jane (*as Sue*) Hello Harold. (*Pause.*) Harold?

Rufus (*as Harold*) What, Sue?

Jane (*as Sue*) Do you think I'm sexy? (*Pause.*) Say 'Hello, sexy Sue'.

Rufus (*as Harold*) Hello sexy Sue.

Jane (*as Sue*) You can kiss me if you like.

The puppets kiss.

Janet's *House*

Janet *is playing with her CB radio.*

Voice Janet! Janet!

Janet What?

Voice Lyndsay's on the phone!

Janet I'm not friends with her. We've fallen out.

Voice What do I tell her?

Janet I'm not speaking to her.

Janet *continues to listen to CB.* **Rufus** *and* **Jane** *play puppets.* **Darrell** *plays his Casio.* **Billy** *is still waiting.*

Victor's *House*

Victor *enters in coat.*

Victor (*to* **Billy**) My mam says we've got to go out now to see my grandma so you'll have to go.

Ushers him out. Shuts door. Takes off his coat. Smiles.

In the Park, Saturday

Hannah *is waiting for* **Bernard**. **Janet** *is sat with her. She has a ball of string which leads out of sight.*

Hannah I don't think he can be coming.

Janet He might have got knocked down.

Hannah Don't say that.

Janet Well he might. He's half an hour late at least. I've been round the park twice since I saw you. While you're sitting here he might be in hospital.

Hannah Thanks.

Janet Do you think he's changed his mind about going out with you?

Hannah No.

Pause.

Janet (*shouting, off*) Trixie! Trixie come over here! (*She pulls on the string.*) She nearly got pregnant last year. This dog got on her and when I kicked it, it was our Trixie that yelped. We had to get a bucket from the bowling green but by the time we'd filled it up from the drinking fountain, they'd finished. (*Pause.*)

Lyndsay rang us up last night, trying to make friends.

Hannah You shouldn't fall out. Now you're going to miss the party.

Janet I know.

Hannah I went to see Wendy last night.

Janet Is she better?

Hannah Not much. She's not allowed in the kitchen now when her Mum's cooking.

Janet No. She ought to have a microwave like what we've got. Then there wouldn't be so many pots and pans to knock over.

Hannah It wouldn't be as dangerous, would it?

Janet No.

Bernard *appears, out of breath.*

Bernard You're here.

Hannah Hello Bernard.

Janet You're nearly an hour late! Just where do you think you've been?

Bernard I got made late. Some kids wanted a fight so I give 'em one.

Janet Oh.

Hannah Are you all right?

Bernard Course I am.

Janet I'm off, then, see you.

She walks off, winding the ball of string as she goes.

Hannah Bye, Janet. (*To* **Bernard**.) What happened?

Bernard I went to the wrong park.

Hannah Oh, Bernard.

Bernard I jogged it here in fifteen minutes and twenty-three seconds.

Hannah Is that good?

Bernard Brilliant.

Hannah Where are we going, then?

Bernard *collapses on the bench.*

A field

Victor *and* **Billy** *enter.* **Billy** *is carrying a large board.*

Billy I'm Indiana Jones and you're that woman chained up over the fire, right.

Billy *holds up* **Victor**'s *arms for him to be the chained woman. He complies, bored.*

And I'm in this cave and the roof is coming down.

Lies on the floor with the board over him.

Aaah, the roof's coming down. Hold on, I'll get my bullwhip.

Cracks the whip.

Got to reach the switch before I'm crushed to death. Done it!

Pushes up the board, slowly, rolls quickly out of the way. Gets up and dusts himself down.

Close shave. Oh no!

He sees an army advancing on him, begins to fight them off.

Victor Aaaaaaaah!

Billy (*startled, no longer acting*) What's up?

Victor Nothing. I'm burning.

Billy Oh. (*Carries on fighting.*)

Victor *gets bored and puts his arms down.*

Billy What are you doing?

Victor My arms are aching.

Billy You're spoiling it.

Victor Let's go down to our den.

Billy It's too far.

They sit. **Billy** *gets out an envelope.*

I'm doing my jigsaw.

He takes out scraps of a picture from a girlie magazine and starts to fit them together.

Victor What are you getting Lyndsay for a present?

Billy Sweets. (*Pause.*) Is that her arm?

Victor Leg. You should have stuck her down on a bit of card.

Billy Yes, but I like fitting all the bits together. I can save the best bits till last. (*Pause.*) What are you getting her?

Victor Sweets. I've got Wendy a get-well present too.

Billy What?

Victor Sweets.

Billy Is she still bad?

Victor I think so. (*Pause.*) I used to go to their house.

Billy What happened?

Victor Nothing. Her mum was really nice, like she was always pleased to see us. I remember playing Cluedo and her mum was sat watching us and she started crying.

Billy What for?

Victor I don't know. I pretended not to notice, but this tear went plop, right on the lid of the box.

Pause.

Billy There, finished. What do you think of her?

Victor Let's have a look. She's got one bigger than the other. (*He blows all the bits away.*)

Billy Oi!

Victor Come on, let's go.

Billy Where?

Victor Let's go to the den.

Billy (*collecting and putting away the bits*) Hang on. Hey, you be in the den, right, as a vietcong, and I'll be Rambo and bomb you with a grenade. (*Demonstrates.*)

Victor It's always me.

Billy I let you be He-Man up at the allotments.

Victor You're not bombing me with bricks. (*Runs off.*)

Billy Where you off?

Victor I'm off to ambush you.

Billy *machineguns him.*

I'm not ready yet!

The Park

Hannah *is writing on the bench.*

Hannah Hannah for Bernard.

Bernard *looks.*

Bernard You don't spell it like that, do you?

Hannah What?

Bernard Hannah.

Hannah Course you do.

Bernard Oh.

Hannah Why?

Bernard I've spelt it different.

Hannah Where?

Bernard I tattooed it on my leg last night.

Hannah You haven't. Can I have a look?

Bernard No.

Hannah Go on.

She chases him off.

Lyndsay's *House*

Lyndsay *is setting out a table with food. There are balloons, cards. Music is playing. Whilst she is getting things ready we see:*

Billy's *House*

Billy *and* **Linda** *are sat facing each other across a table.* **Billy** *has a plate in front of him with dinner on it.*

Rufus's *Cousin's House*

Rufus *and* **Jane** *are busy having a Sue and Harold conversation.*

Lyndsay *has now moved out of her party room.*

Janet's *House*

Voice Janet!

Janet (*into her CB*) 10.6 Hold on a minute. (*To* **Voice**.) What?

Voice Lyndsay's on the phone again.

Janet All right. I'm coming. (*To CB*.) I've got to go. Pick you up later. (*Pause*.) 10.4. This is Dolly signing off. Over and out.

She goes off.

Billy's *House*

Linda Swallow it!

Billy *shakes his head, rolls something disgusting round his mouth.*

You're not moving until you've eaten it. I mean it, Billy. If I have to sit here all night, you're going to eat it. You little sod, stop being a baby.

She makes a move to him. He spits out part of a sausage onto the plate, tries to get away but she grabs him by the hair, pulls his head back and in goes the sausage again. They sit facing each other again, both almost in tears.

You asked me for sausages, Billy. What's wrong with them?

Hannah's House

Hannah *is putting the final touches to her party outfit in front of a mirror.* **Darrell** *enters.*

Darrell Hannah.

He taps her on the shoulder.

Hey, you look nice.

Hannah Do I? Really? Thanks, Darrell. (*Kisses him.*)

Darrell Have a good time.

Hannah I will.

Darrell Mam says half eleven.

Hannah She said half ten.

Darrell She says half eleven now. Bernard's downstairs.

She rushes off.

Lyndsay's House

Victor *is the first to arrive. He gives her a present.*

Lyndsay (*kissing him*) Oh, thank you, Victor.

She shows him to a chair by the food table.

Won't be a minute.

Moves off. **Victor** *picks up a goodie to eat.*

Lyndsay (*her back to him*) Don't eat anything.

She goes. **Victor** *puts the goodie back on the plate.*

Billy's *House*

Linda Go on, then, get off to your party!

Billy *shoots out of the room.*

The Party

'Star-trekking' is on the cassette player. **Janet** *and* **Lyndsay** *are doing a silly dance together.*

Victor *is laid on the floor with his mouth open,* **Billy** *is a dive bomber trying to hit the target of* **Victor**'s *mouth with nuts.* **Bernard** *and* **Hannah** *are smooch-waltzing. The song ends.* **Lyndsay** *picks up a letter, goes over to* **Hannah** *with it.*

Lyndsay Hannah, will you put this somewhere or you'll forget to take it to Wendy.

A slow waltz begins. **Bernard** *and* **Hannah** *sit down.* **Janet** *grabs* **Billy**, **Lyndsay** *grabs* **Victor**. *They dance.* **Billy** *tries to escape but* **Janet** *holds him tight to her.*

Billy I'm suffocating! I can't breathe!

Wendy's *House*

Wendy *is reading a letter.*

Lyndsay Dear Wendy, we thought we would write you a letter because you are poorly and can't come to my party.

Hannah We have thought of a good idea what we would like to do to help you and your mum.

Bernard We thought it would be a good idea to do some

sponsored things to raise some money to buy your mum a microwave oven.

Janet Janet thought of the oven because it's safer than pots and pans.

Billy Any money left over we will give to the school as our leaving present because this is our last term. This is Billy's idea.

Victor If you would like us to do some sponsored things and your mum says it's OK, please sign on the dotted line and return to Hannah. Love from –

They say their names in turn.

PS Hope you like the sweets. Get well soon.

Billy's *House, Later*

Darkness.

Billy (*singing*) Happy birthday to you, squashed tomatoes and stew. Bread and butter, in the gutter, happy birthday to you.

Linda Billy! Shut up and get to sleep!

Back to School. The Playground

All are gathered around **Hannah**.

Janet Come on, what did she say?

Hannah She said yes. Look, one from Wendy and one from her mum.

Shows letters, all excited.

Janet I'm doing a sponsored dog walk!

Bernard I'll do running.

Billy Yeah.

Victor Yeah, we'll do running.

Bernard You'll have to do some training.

Lyndsay I'll do dancing.

Victor Hey, I'll do dancing with you.

Hannah You'll all have to help me organise it.

Janet Teachers will help. We'll ask them. They're getting some of the money, aren't they?

Bernard Rufus? What can you do?

Rufus I can't do anything.

Bernard There must be something you can do.

Rufus There isn't anything I can do.

Janet There must be.

Rufus Well I can't think what it is.

Billy You'll have to do something.

Rufus Do I have to?

They all chorus 'yes' etc. The bell goes.

Drama Lesson

Billy Miss, can we do a play about robbing banks?

Janet You're always doing plays about robbing banks. Miss, can we do one about . . . I've forgot now!

Hannah Can we do families?

Janet Yes. Families going on holiday.

Suddenly **Janet** *and* **Hannah** *spring up and start organising their 'families'.*

Victor What are we doing?

Billy (*sick*) We're doing a women's play.

Victor What have we got to do, Miss?

Janet Family arguments. You're my husband. (*To* **Lyndsay**.) You're my daughter.

Victor I'm not being your husband. I want to be Hannah's husband.

Janet Bernard's going to be Hannah's husband, aren't you, Bernard?

Lyndsay *and* **Janet** *'Ooooh' at this remark.*

Hannah Will you be my husband?

Janet To have and to hold.

Lyndsay From this day forward.

Bernard I can't, can I? I've got to go in a minute.

They organise themselves into two families.

Hannah – *Mum,* **Victor** – *Dad,* **Billy** – *Son.*

Rufus – *Dad,* **Janet** – *Mum,* **Lyndsay** – *Daughter.*

Janet We're ready to start working it out now, Miss.

Hannah We're ready, Miss.

Each group goes into a huddle. **Bernard** *bring his chair forward. Sits.*

Bernard's *Careers Interview*

Bernard No, Miss, I'm only missing drama. When I was in Sheffield the PE teacher used to say that drama stood for dance, run, and muck about.

(*Reading.*) Bernard Easley, 14 St Peter's Road.

Mother – cleaner. Father – decorator.

My career ideas – Army.

(*Looking up.*) Yes, Miss, paratroopers.

(*Reading.*) My work experience – I worked at Snitterby's butchers from December 7th to 14th, last year.

(*Looking up.*) It was good. It built my muscles up lifting the meat.

I've got a paper round and I might be getting a Saturday job on the market.

I went to the army careers office like you said and I had a sort of interview and filled in a form and now I'm just waiting to get a letter to go down to Aldershot for a trial.

(*Reading.*) Personal likes – Sport, martial arts films.

(*Looking up.*) I like all sports, Miss. Boxing? (*Unsure.*) Yes, I like boxing. My dad got me interested.

Dad's voice Hey! Hey!

Bernard What?

Voice Don't what me. Who do you think you're talking to?

Bernard My dad.

Voice Come here.

Bernard I'm busy, Dad.

Victor *gets up from the huddle and acts as* **Bernard**'s *dad.*

Dad (*thumping him on the arm*) What's she like, then?

Bernard Who?

Dad This bird. What's she called?

Bernard Hannah.

Dad (*thumping*) What's she like?

Bernard Don't, Dad.

Dad (*mimicking*) 'Don't Dad'. Come on. (*Thumps.*) What's she like?

Bernard All right.

Dad All right at snogging.

Bernard Dad.

Dad She given you any lovebites?

Bernard Leave off.

Dad You want to get cracking instead of sitting in here thinking about it.

Victor *returns to his group.*

Bernard I just want to travel, Miss. I don't want to stay here any more.

Drama Lesson

Janet Miss, can we go first?

Hannah's *group move back.* **Janet, Rufus** *and* **Lyndsay** *take up their positions.* **Rufus** *reads a paper, smokes pipe,* **Janet** *knits.* **Lyndsay** *is offstage.*

Janet (*as Mum*) Where the bloody hell has she got to? (*As* *herself.*) Ooops. Sorry, Miss. (*As Mum.*) What time is it now? (*Pause. She whispers to* **Rufus** *who is oblivious, reading his pretend paper. As herself.*) Miss, he's supposed to say half past eleven, he's not doing it properly.

Rufus I don't know what I'm supposed to say. I don't even know what I'm doing. You never told me.

Janet Miss, I did tell him but he never listens. (*To* **Rufus**.) Start again. (*As Mum.*) Where has she got to?

Rufus (*as Dad*) It's half past eleven.

Janet Oh, Miss, he can't do it. Can we have Bernard? Come on, Bernard.

Bernard *replaces* **Rufus**. **Janet** *whispers instructions in his ear.*

The play proper begins.

Janet (*as Mum*) Where's she got to? What time is it now?

Bernard (*as Dad*) Half past eleven.

Janet (*as Mum*) Anything could have happened to her. She could have got mugged or raped or anything.

Bernard (*as Dad*) I'll mug her when she gets in. Just you wait.

Knock on door. Suddenly **Victor**'*s hand shoots up.*

Victor Miss, you don't knock on your own door.

Janet (*savagely, at* **Victor**) She forgot her key!

Bernard (*to* **Lyndsay**) Get in here! (*Thumps and pushes her.*) What time do you call this?

Lyndsay My watch stopped.

Bernard (*thumping her*) Watch stopped. A likely story. Don't lie to me.

Lyndsay I'm not lying.

Janet I've been worrying my soul case out over you, young lady.

Lyndsay I'm sick of you. You never let me do anything.

Bernard Don't talk to your mother like that.

Lyndsay I'll talk how I want. I'm eighteen. I'll do what I want.

Bernard (*thumping her*) While you're living in my house you'll do as I say.

Lyndsay Well I'm going to leave home and get a flat.

Bernard You do that. Then we might get some peace. Now get to bed! (*Pushes her off.*)

Lyndsay (*as herself*) I haven't finished yet, I've got some more to do.

Bernard (*almost without a pause*) Don't argue with me, sit down!

Other group start to laugh. **Bernard** *and* **Janet** *have lost the thread.*

Janet Miss, we went wrong. That's it.

The other group clap then jump up to take their positions. **Janet**, **Bernard**, **Lyndsay** *sit and watch.*

Lyndsay (*to* **Bernard**) You hurt me.

Bernard Sorry.

Hannah, **Victor** *and* **Billy** *begin their play. A melodramatic idea, but they put a great deal of emotion into it. It concerns* **Billy** *finding out accidentally that he is adopted. A row ensues. Mother cries. Dad tells Son that he was adopted because Mother couldn't have children as a result of being raped when she was little. It finishes with* **Billy** *apologising. All three are magically caught up and are crying.*

Hannah That's it, Miss.

Janet, Bernard, Lyndsay *clap, stand and come forward. All stand in a line, facing the front.*

Miss, have you had a think about what we asked you this morning? (*Pause.*) All of us, Miss.

Bernard Yeah, all of us want to do something to show people what we can do. We might be thick but there are some things we are good at.

Janet I'm not thick.

Bernard Yes, you are. We all are.

Janet I'm not thick. My mam says I'm special. We're special aren't we, Miss? See? It's just you that's thick.

Bernard Shurrup. We could do all the events in one day. I'll organise training.

Hannah I'll make out all the sponsor forms, Miss, if you show me how to do it.

Victor Please, Miss, let us do it. We'll work it all out properly. We could get a lot of money, couldn't we?

Billy Yes, hundreds. Get a microwave for Wendy and a computer for the school.

Pause.

Bernard We WOULD collect all the money in, wouldn't we?

Chorus of 'yes'.

Lyndsay It would be our leaving present for the school as well as for Wendy. Please, Miss.

Pause. All erupt in a yell of delight and 'Thanks, Miss'. They all leave, except for **Rufus**.

Rufus Have you got any jobs, Miss? (*Pause.*) Goodnight.
Walks off.

In the Corridor

Bernard *is waiting for* **Rufus**.

Rufus I can't do anything.

Bernard Yes you can.

Rufus I'll make a mess of it.

Bernard What?

Rufus Anything. I always do.

They go off.

Getting in some Training

Lyndsay*'s House:* **Lyndsay** *is dancing to music.*

In the Park: **Billy** *enters, does step ups on the bench.*

In the Street: **Janet** *enters with her ball of string which leads off out of sight.*

Janet Come on! Heel! Heel! (*She tries to wind in.*) Trixie!
(*She goes back the way she came.*)

Bernard*'s House:* **Bernard** *is doing exercises.*

Victor*'s House:* **Victor** *is praying.*

Victor Our Father, who art in heaven, please make people
sponsor us for a lot of money and let us try really hard at

whatever it is we are doing and do a good job for Wendy and the school. I've made everybody promise to help each other.

Mrs Anderson, our teacher, has said we can do the things when it's our sports day and we can have an open evening on the same night and sell things. Hannah and Janet and Lyndsay are making some cakes. Please will you help Rufus to think of something. Amen.

Rufus's *Cousin's House*

Rufus *has Harold.* **Jane** *has a skipping rope and Sue.*

Rufus (*as Harold*) What are you going to do with that rope?

Jane (*as Sue*) I'm going to tie you up to this tree.

She takes his free hand and Harold and starts to tie them both to a bar.

Rufus (*as Harold*) What are you doing that for?

Jane (*as Sue*) I'm going to rob your house.

Rufus (*as Harold*) Help! Help!

Jane (*as Sue*) Keep quiet.

She stuffs a handkerchief in Harold's mouth.

Rufus (*as Harold*) Mmm mm mmmm.

Jane *makes police car noises and gets up.*

Rufus (*as Harold*) Where are you going?

Jane (*as Sue*) I can hear a police car. I'm going.

She goes off.

Rufus (*as himself*) Hang on. Jane! Come back, Jane!
Struggles unsuccessfully to free himself.

Billy'*s House*

Billy Put down fifty pence a lap.

Linda How many laps can you do?

Billy About fifty.

Linda One p a lap.

Billy Oh, come on, it's for a good cause.

Linda Five p.

Billy Done.

Linda This isn't a proper form. You've written this.

Billy I know. I'll put it on the proper form when we get
them. Can you take my form to the hairdressers and get all
your customers to sign it?

Linda No.

Billy Well your work mates, then?

Linda I'll see.

Billy Get your boyfriend to put down twenty p a lap and I
promise not to keep coming in when you're on the sofa.

Hannah's *House*

Darrell I'm on the dole, aren't I?

Hannah I'm only asking you for fifty p at the most.

Darrell Why can't Bernard ask me?

Hannah Because I'm asking you.

Darrell How come my mam's sponsoring him when he ant even got his own mam and dad down here?

Hannah Because I've only just written his form out. Come on.

Darrell I might be buying that Casio off my mate.

Hannah You're a Scrooge.

Darrell We haven't even got a microwave oursens!

Hannah *won't give in. He signs.*

Two p a lap.

She kisses him.

Darrell You ought to be getting sponsored for the number of people you can con money out of.

Janet's *House*

Voice Janet! Open this door!

Janet No!

Voice What have you done with Trixie? Janet! Janet will you open this door!

Janet, *upset, starts singing to herself.*

Have you lost her? I told you not to take her out when

she's coming into season. Which one was it? That bloody Jack Russell, I bet! Well, you can forget your dog walk. Do you hear me? I said you can forget your dog walk!

Janet *is now 'la la'-ing her way through a song, loudly.*

Rufus*'s Cousin's House*

Rufus *is still tied up.*

Rufus Jane! Aunty Maureen? Somebody!

Later, at the Flat of a **Young Woman**

The **Young Woman** *is sat, drinking coffee from a mug. A baby can be heard crying. There is a knock at the door. She gets up and goes off.*

Bernard*'s voice* Hello. My name is Bernard Easley. I go to St Peter's Special School and I'm doing a sponsored run to raise money for the school and to help a girl who has fits. It's for a good cause. She had a fit in the kitchen –

Young Woman*'s voice* Come in.

They both come into the room. She picks up her empty coffee cup.

What do you want?

Bernard I'm sorry, I haven't got time for a drink. I've got to get round all the other flats.

Young Woman No. What do you want?

Bernard (*starting again*) I'm doing a sponsored run to raise money for my school and –

Young Woman How much do you want?

Bernard What you like. Thank you.

Young Woman Twenty p?

Bernard Thank you.

The **Young Woman** *goes off.* **Bernard** *stands listening to the baby. The* **Young Woman** *comes back with her purse. She offers him the money.*

Bernard No. I mean I haven't done it yet. You have to give me it after I've done it in a couple of weeks. I'll put your name down. I've got a pen.

The **Young Woman** *takes paper, writes name.*

It's only a rough copy. I'll come back with a proper one. (*Pause.*) Is that a boy or a girl?

Young Woman Boy.

She gives him the paper back.

Bernard Thank you very much. I'll be seeing you, then.

He goes out. The **Young Woman** *goes off to see to the baby.*

Another Flat

Victor *and* **Billy** *come forward.* **Victor** *mimes ringing a bell.*

Voice What?

Victor We're from St Peter's school and we're doing a sponsored thing to –

Voice Clear off.

Victor We're raising money –

Voice I'm not interested.

Billy Penny a lap for me.

Victor Penny an hour for me.

Voice What do I get out of it?

Victor Nothing.

Voice Well clear off, then.

Door slams.

Billy Get stuffed.

Victor Yeah, get stuffed.

They pull faces at the door.

Games Lesson. On the School Field

All are in PE gear. **Billy, Victor** *are training with the help of* **Bernard. Hannah, Lyndsay** *and* **Janet** *are at the high jump pits.* **Rufus** *is raking the sand.*

Hannah Why don't you do sponsored cake eating?

Janet I'm too fat already.

Lyndsay You're not fat.

Janet I am.

Lyndsay You're not. I am.

Janet I'm fatter than you.

Lyndsay Yes, but that's because you're smaller. If I was as small as you I'd be as fat as you.

Janet Thanks.

Rufus *has wandered over to* **Bernard**.

Rufus Bernard?

Bernard What?

Rufus I've got an idea.

Bernard Carry on, lads. (*Moves off a little with* **Rufus**.) What?

Rufus Sponsored escapology.

Bernard You what?

Rufus I get sponsored for how long it takes me to escape from having my hands and legs tied together and being put into a sack. (*Pause.*) The longer it takes me, the less they have to pay.

Pause.

Bernard Can we put you in a tank of water?

Rufus I can't swim.

Bernard You're thick! (*Walks off back to his training duties.*)

Victor (*exhausted*) Bernard, I wanted to ask you if I can change from running to dancing.

Bernard *glares.*

It's all right. I haven't got any sponsors yet so it won't matter. I think I want to do a dancing marathon now instead if you don't mind. I'm sorry.

Bernard *is furious. He storms off in disgust.*

Rufus *'s Careers Interview*

Rufus (*reading*) Russell Croft, 127 Westerdale Avenue.
Mother – housewife.

My career ideas –

(*Looking up.*) Miss, you told me to leave it blank until we
thought of something.

(*Reading.*) My work experience – absent from Friday 4th
December till end of autumn term. Se – se – (*Looks up.*)
Miss, I can't read this. (*Shows paper.*) Severe. Severe nose
bleeds.

(*Looks up.*) I had a place at the crisp factory, Miss, but I
started to get nervous about starting and that started my
nose bleeds.

(*Reading.*) Courses – none.

Personal likes – collecting shells.

(*Looks up.*) I've got lots, Miss. My great grandma used to
live at Sewerby near Bridlington and I got them from near
there. She's dead now. I make sculptures with them
sometimes. You use a really fine drill and you drill a real
tiny hole through the shell and then you can thread them
together with fine wire or nylon if you're making a
necklace. I make puppets as well, Miss, out of socks.

I still don't know what I could do, Miss. A jeweller?
Would they let me do that?

The Playground

Hannah *is lecturing the gang.*

Hannah Now look, we're not giving in. Bernard is trying
as hard as he can and we're not helping him. You've made

him real mad. We've all got to try hard. We CAN get the
ideas going and we can get the money raised.

Billy You're not doing anything.

Hannah I'm organising it. And I'm cooking, right? Right,
Billy. You're still doing your running round the school
field. There's your form. Victor, you're doing an eight
hour dance marathon.

Victor Eight hours? Is that all? That's easy.

Hannah Mrs Anderson says you're not allowed to do any
more. Here. (*Gives him form.*) Change it from running to
dancing. Janet. You're cooking and being the DJ.

Victor The what?

Janet DJ. Disc Jockey. I'm going to be playing all your
music.

Hannah Lyndsay's mum won't let her do the dancing but
she's going to do some cooking and she's doing Madonna.

Victor Madonna? How can you get sponsored for that?

Billy They pay her to shut up.

Lyndsay You shut up you midget.

Hannah It's all part of the entertainment. She's good at
Madonna. Right. Rufus?

They all look at him.

Rufus I'm going to make some jewellery to sell and some
puppets.

Pause as they take this in.

Hannah That's a good idea, Rufus, well done. Well then,
are we still going to do it?

Chorus of 'Yes'.

Are we going to do it?

(*With great enthusiasm.*) Yeah!

Outside a House

Bernard *and* **Hannah** *appear.*

Bernard Come on, you can do this one.

Hannah No.

Bernard Come on.

Hannah No, Bernard, don't make me.

Bernard You'll be OK. Just take your time.

Hannah I can't.

Bernard What you coming round with me for, then?

Hannah Because you're my boyfriend. Because I want to be with you. Don't you want me with you?

Bernard You never say anything when they answer the door. You just stand there looking gormless. Try to talk to people.

Hannah It's too difficult. (*She looks down.*)

Bernard *rings bell. We hear voices in* **Hannah**'s *head* –

Hannah Stop making fun of me.

Voice 1 (*mimicking*) Stop making fun of me.

Voice 2 (*mimicking*) She can't help the way she talks.

Voice 1 Hannah! (*Mimicking.*) Where's your funny voice gone?

Voice 2 Have you lost it?

Bernard *rings bell again, steps back as door is opened, giving* **Hannah** *the spot.*

Hannah Hello. I'm Hannah O'Brien and I go to St Peter's special school. (*Again.*) I'm Hannah O'Brien. (*Again.*) Hannah O'Brien. (*She looks to* **Bernard** *for help.*)

We're doing some sponsored events to raise money for our school and for a microwave. (*Again, as carefully as she can.*) Microwave oven. This girl has epileptic fits. (*Again.*) Epileptic fits. (*In agony, again.*) Epileptic fits!

She turns and runs off, crying.

Bernard Sorry. (*Runs after her.*) Hannah!

The Park

Victor *is sat on the bench, with radio playing. He is tapping his feet to the music. Gradually gets more of his body into the music.*

Voice 1 Hello, Victor, what you doing?

Victor I'm waiting for my friend. He's running round the park.

Voice 1 What for?

Victor He's in training. He's running, I'm dancing. We're doing it to raise money.

Voice 2 Can you dance?

Voice 1 Course he can, can't you?

Victor Course I can.

Voice 2 Go on, let's see you.

Victor I only do it for money.

Voice 1 Are you a professional dancer?

Victor Nearly.

Voice 2 Will you dance with me?

Victor All right. (*Gets up.*) It'll cost you two p.

Mimes taking money.

It's for a good cause.

Dances.

Voice 1 Hey, Victor, that's brilliant.

He dances for a while. Music suddenly stops.

Victor What have you done that for?

Voice 1 We're off to get some of our mates to come and see you.

Voice 2 Yeah, they'll want to see you. They'll pay a lot of money to see you dancing.

Victor Will they?

Voice 1 Yeah. See you in a minute. Wait here.

Victor Right. See you.

He sits back on the bench.

Janet's *House*

Janet *is on her CB.*

Janet She's called Trixie. She's medium-sized and scruffy-looking. She's got brown and black and grey and white under her neck. Yes, she's got a collar on. She might have some string fastened on it because it broke. She's in season.

Crackling response from other end.

Hey, are you coming to our school open evening? On Friday. I'm going to be the DJ.

Crackling response.

Hannah's *House*

Darrell *is playing on the Casio.* **Lyndsay** *is stood by him, fascinated. She is carrying a tape recorder.* **Darrell** *finishes, waits for response.*

Lyndsay That was really good, wasn't it?

Darrell Thanks.

He tinkers with the keys, not really making any music.

Lyndsay I'd better go. If she's out with Bernard she won't be back till later, will she? I thought she might be in.

Darrell OK.

Lyndsay Are you in a band?

Darrell Eh? Just getting started, really. Need a bit more practice. Only done a couple of gigs.

Lyndsay You're good. What are you called?

Darrell Er . . . we're changing our name. We want something a bit more streetwise than what we had.

Lyndsay What was it?

Darrell Oh, it was crap.

Lyndsay What?

Darrell Morning Becomes Electric.

Lyndsay Oh.

Darrell I said it was crap. My mate got it from a book.

Pause.

What are you doing for this thing then, this what Hannah's doing?

Lyndsay I'm doing some singing.

Darrell Oh, yeah? What sort of stuff?

Lyndsay Madonna. I just sing along with the record.

Darrell Can you sing?

Lyndsay Not very well.

Darrell I bet. Is that what the tape is? Madonna?

Lyndsay I was going to ask Hannah if she'd watch me to see if it was all right.

Darrell Come on, then.

Lyndsay No!

Darrell Why not?

Lyndsay I'm embarrassed.

Darrell Look, you're doing it on stage in front of people, aren't you?

Lyndsay I'm not doing it for you.

Darrell I can tell you if it's any good. I'm a musician, aren't I? (*Pause.*) You might be what we need for the band.

Lyndsay I can't! Oh no! Your band? Oh, no!

Darrell *takes tape recorder, switches it on. Madonna.*

Don't watch me! Turn around and let me get started and then you can.

He turns around. She begins. He turns to watch her. Suddenly **Hannah** *rushes in, upset.* **Darrell** *turns off the tape.*

Lyndsay Hannah, what's happened?

Hannah He made me talk! He showed me up, he made me talk!

Lyndsay Bernard?

Hannah Yes. (*Pause.*) What you doing?

Lyndsay I was just showing him what I'm going to be doing. He was telling me about his band.

Darrell *goes out.*

It's all right, Hannah.

Hannah Why did he make me do it? He can't love me if he can do that.

The Park

We hear 'I Heard It through the Grapevine'. **Victor** *is dancing on the bench. He has taken off his shirt and is now taking off his trousers.*

Voice I bet he drinks Carling Black Label!

Lots of 'Oooh's' from girls' voices. **Billy** *runs in.*

Billy What are you doing?

Victor I've got £1.20.

Young Woman's *Flat*

The **Young Woman** *is putting washing into a plastic bag. A knock. She goes off.*

Bernard's *voice* I've come about this sheet you've filled in.

Young Woman's *voice* Come in.

They enter.

Bernard He's not crying.

Young Woman I was just going down to the launderette. I'll have to wake him up.

Bernard I thought I'd better see you about this form. I said about filling in a proper sheet, well I've got one, but before you fill it in I thought I'd better tell you that I think twenty p a lap is too much because I'm going to be doing a good few laps and I don't want it costing you a lot of money. We all need what money we can get nowadays, don't we? Specially when you've got a baby to look after. (*Pause.*) So if you put, say, ten p a lap then it won't cost you more than about one pound fifty. That's quite enough I think, don't you?

She signs form.

I don't want your husband after me for making you give your housekeeping away, do I?

She gives him the form back.

Is he at work?

Young Woman I don't now. We're not married.

Bernard Do you work?

Young Woman No.

Bernard No. (*Pause.*) You see, I might do as many as

twenty-five laps. I used to go to Sheffield Harriers. So put five p, eh?

Young Woman You wouldn't do me a favour, would you?

Bernard Yeah. What?

Young Woman Well, you wouldn't stop here while I take this lot, would you? And I'll leave the form as it is, at ten p a lap?

Bernard What if your boyfriend comes back?

Young Woman He won't.

Bernard What if he wakes up?

Young Woman Stick his dummy in the tin of treacle that's on the windowsill. I'm only over the road. Will you?

Bernard All right.

Young Woman Thanks ever so much.

She goes. **Bernard** *starts to look around the flat.*

The Playground

Janet *is stood between* **Hannah** *and* **Bernard**.

Janet Please start talking to each other again, you're making me upset. I don't like it. Say you're sorry to her, Bernard.

Bernard I have.

Janet (*to* **Hannah**) Well make friends, then.

Hannah He didn't come after me, did he? He let me go home on my own.

Bernard She *went* home on her own.

Hannah You should have stopped me.

Bernard I thought you wanted to be on your own.

Janet Stop arguing! Hannah, do you still want to go out with Bernard?

Hannah You'd better ask him if he still wants to go out with me.

Janet Do you still want to go out with Hannah?

Bernard Don't be daft. I do go out with her. She's still my girlfriend. We're just having a tiff.

Janet A what?

Bernard Them tiffs.

Hannah I'm sorry, Bernard.

Bernard No, I'm sorry.

Janet (*as Mum*) Eeeh, young love nowadays. In my day we had to wait till we were married. No hanky panky. (*Pause.*) Hannah, will you take my cooking things, for me? Tell Lyndsay she can start doing the pastry if she wants.

Hannah All right. (*Goes off with* **Bernard**. **Janet** *comes forward.*)

Janet's *Careers Interview*

Janet (*reading*) Janet Proctor, 3 Brentnall Road. Father – taxi driver. Mother – taxi receptionist.

My career ideas – record shop, MacDonalds, telephonist, receptionist, vet, local radio presenter.

(*Looking up.*) Miss, I think Radio Humberside might be coming tomorrow. (*Pause.*) I might be able to talk to somebody about a job. (*Pause.*) I like talking to people, Miss.

(*Reading.*) My work experience – I worked at Dr Barnado's shop from 7th to 14th December, last year. Supervisor, Mrs Owen.

(*Looking up.*) There was this tramp come in every day, Miss, and he kept calling me Miss Moffett. He ponged a bit but he was all right. He never bought anything. We had a few women in, buying clothes and baby things.

(*Reading.*) Courses – RAF, Tech College.

Personal likes – CB radio, horses, dogs, watching TV.

(*Looking up.*) Lyndsay's making cakes and jam tarts, Miss.

Cookery Lesson

Billy *is playing with bits of leftover pastry.* **Lyndsay** *is supervising cooking, etc.* **Hannah** *is cleaning a tray.* **Bernard** *is just sat reading a comic.* **Janet** *puts on her apron and joins them. They chat about cooking temperatures, times, numbers, etc. Suddenly* **Victor** *rushes in.*

Victor Hey! Hey, Miss, guess what?

All What?

Victor You won't believe this. I know I didn't to begin with.

All What?

Victor Guess who might be coming tomorrow?

Billy Victor Sylvester.

Victor No. Yorkshire TV Calendar News!

They all go wild.

Mr Tong says they're going to Cleethorpes to do a murder and if they finish it before two they're stopping off to do us on their way back to Leeds!

Bernard When would we be on telly?

Victor Tomorrow night, I think.

Bernard Will it be like interviewing us?

Victor Yes.

Lyndsay Oh, what will I say? I won't know what to say! Janet, ask me some questions.

Bernard Ask me some.

Janet How do you feel?

Bernard Er . . .

Billy Knackered!

Janet You can't say that! Miss, did you hear him?

Billy We will be, though, won't we?

Bernard What was it again?

Lyndsay They'll want to talk to you, Hannah, won't they?

All Yes. (*'Yes they will', etc.*)

Hannah I'm not talking.

Lyndsay You'll have to. You thought of it.

Hannah I'm not!

Bernard She doesn't have to if she doesn't want.

Janet I'll do it. I'll talk to them. I know all about microphones. (*Pause. They start to pack away.*) (*To* **Hannah**.) We've got to pack away, now.

Lyndsay On telly, eh, Rufus?

Rufus I'm going to see my mum tonight, in hospital.

Lyndsay Tell her to watch Calendar News tomorrow night.

Janet I can't wait to tell my mum.

Bernard We might get a lot more people coming now, if the telly people's there.

Victor On telly. Dancing!

Billy You'll be able to charge double for a strip, now.

They say their goodbyes.

Hannah's *House*

Darrell I told you you should have had our band playing!

Hannah What band?

Darrell Somebody big could be sitting watching telly and there we are. This could have been it.

Hannah You don't know enough songs.

Darrell We've written another two numbers this afternoon!

Billy's *House*

Billy Go on, Linda.

Linda I'm not perming your hair!

Billy Why not?

Linda No.

Billy Oh, why not?

Linda No!

Rufus's *Cousin's House*

Jane *is putting a scuba face mask on* **Rufus**'s *face.*

Jane Breathe deeply. It's only gas to put you to sleep, it won't hurt.

She lays him down, then gets out a penknife.

Rufus (*sitting up*) I'm not playing.

Jane Let me get the baby out.

Rufus No, I'm not playing!

Jane You'll go septic.

Rufus No!

Jane (*getting up*) Well get lost, then! (*Pause.*) I'll be glad when you've gone back to your own house. You're boring. My mam says she's getting fed up of you, too. Feeding you and taking you to the hospital. You can't even be bothered to say 'thank you' to her. And she told me you wet the bed.

Rufus No I don't. She didn't say that.

Jane Yes she did. You piss yourself. You can't even be bothered to use the toilet. She's even had to buy a plastic sheet!

Jane *goes.* **Rufus** *takes off his mask. He picks up a female puppet, puts it on his hand.*

Rufus (*as Mum*) Russell. Give your mum a big kiss. (*He does.*) I'll be coming home soon. Don't worry about me. How's school?

(*As himself.*) We're doing our sponsored sports day tomorrow. Television might be there.

(*As Mum.*) Oh, Russell. Are you going to be on television?

(*As himself.*) Yes, Mum.

(*As Mum.*) Nurse! Did you hear that, nurse? My son's going to be on television!

(*As himself.*) Shut up, Mum. (*Pause.*) I love you.

The Park, Later

Janet, **Hannah** *and* **Lyndsay** *are sat on the park bench, singing together. They stop, listening to the night.*

Hannah I like stars.

Lyndsay I do. I've got a lucky star outside my bedroom window.

Janet My mam told me that God put stars in the sky to stop us being afraid of the dark. That's why I sleep with my curtains open.

Hannah I do.

Lyndsay I do. (*Pause.*) I'm not going to be able to sleep, tonight.

Janet I'm not.

Lyndsay Wendy's mum is ace, isn't she?

Janet She's funny.

Hannah She thinks you're funny.

Lyndsay She never stopped thanking me.

Janet Nor me.

Hannah She wouldn't let go of me, would she?

Lyndsay Hey, Hannah?

Hannah What?

Lyndsay Janet?

Janet What?

Lyndsay (*holding their hands*) Ace mates! We're going to stay mates after we've left school, aren't we?

Janet Course.

Hannah Course.

Lyndsay Hannah?

Hannah What?

Lyndsay Can I be bridesmaid at your and Bernard's wedding?

Janet Can I?

Hannah Course. We're best friends, aren't we?

They sing themselves off home.

The **Young Woman**'s *Flat*

A knock.

Bernard's *voice* Hello, I've just come to tell you I might be on television tomorrow night about this thing I'm doing.

Young Woman's *voice* Oh, will you? Great.

Bernard's *voice* I think we're going to get a lot of people there. Do you want to come?

Young Woman's *voice* I can't. He's come back.

Bernard's *voice* Oh.

Young Woman's *voice* I'll watch you on telly, eh?

Bernard's *voice* Will you?

Young Woman's *voice* Promise. I'll have to go.

Victor's *House*

Victor Dear God, it's me again. Please make me go to sleep. My mam says I've got to have ten hours if I'm dancing all day. (*Pause.*) Everything's going to be great, isn't it?

Day of Events

Billy *and* **Bernard** *are in their shorts, limbering up on the line.* **Hannah** *has a table next to them with orange, cups, lap-counter.* **Janet** *and* **Lyndsay** *are wandering the crowd with trays of cakes. In the Hall* **Victor** *is waiting to start his dance marathon.* **Rufus** *is his official timekeeper.*

Loud Hailer (*whine*) One. Two. (*Blow.*) Good morning everyone. It's lovely to see so many parents here today on this our very special sports day for a very special school. I'm sure you don't need reminding that our Fifth Years are making today a very important day. Please support their efforts, not just by cheering but also by visiting the stalls and buying some of the cakes made by the girls and Mrs Smart of our cookery department.

Janet We made these!

Lyndsay We made all of them!

Loud Hailer I've got two of the Fifth Year girls waving at me. Yes, girls. Cake trays are coming round. Thank you, girls.

Girls Wooooh!

Loud Hailer I'd like to start off events today with the marathon run by our two Fifth Year boys Bernard Easley and William Starkey.

Girls Haaay!

Loud Hailer Also, at the same time, I'd like to start off the eight hour dance marathon by Victor Gilbey, who is in our school hall right now, and should be able to hear me give the signal to start. Can you hear me in the hall?

Victor and **Rufus** *wave and shout.*

Is there anybody there? I can't see you. Oh, yes. Do pay Victor a visit during the day – and tonight if you are coming along to our open evening. He's got a very official visiting book for you to sign. I am assured that it is needed for official timekeeping.

Rufus Me! Russell Croft! Russell Croft! Timekeeper!

Loud Hailer Right, then, ladies and gentlemen, boys and girls, let me just consult my deputies a moment and we'll begin.

Lyndsay (*seeing someone in the crowd*) Hiya!

Voice Hello, Lyndsay, aren't you running?

Janet She can't run in a straight line.

Lyndsay Yes I can.

Janet Do you want a cake? Only five p.

Loud Hailer Right, ladies and gentlemen. Are we ready boys? On your marks, get set, go!

Music on. **Victor** *starts dancing,* **Billy** *and* **Bernard** *set off running.* **Janet** *and* **Lyndsay** *watch a while then continue to sell their cakes.*

Would competitors for the First Year boys' two hundred yards make their way down to Mr Tong?

Rufus *is signing people in and trying to sell his jewellery.*

Billy *and* **Bernard** *come round for the first lap. They wave away* **Hannah***'s offer of a drink.* **Hannah** *puts up 'Lap 1'.*

Victor Rufus?

Rufus What?

Victor I want to go to the toilet.

Rufus Already?

Victor I went three times before I came to school.

Rufus You can't stop dancing.

Victor I'll have to.

Rufus I'll have to come with you.

Victor I want a number two!

Rufus I'll stand outside. You'll have to keep moving your arms and legs to the music.

They go off. **Victor** *takes the tape with him.*

Lyndsay How many have you sold?

Janet I'm going to have to go in for my second trayful in a minute.

Lyndsay Don't keep eating them, Janet!

Janet I'm not, I'm selling them!

Loud Hailer Will those boys keep back off the track, please, behind the rope? First Year girls' hundred yards to Mr Tong.

Hannah Come on, Bernard! Come on, Billy!

As they pass her she holds out a drink for them. She runs alongside them till finished. Moves the lap counter to 'Lap 4'.

Billy I'm not going to make twenty laps.

Bernard You will. Stop thinking about it. Think about something else.

Billy My feet hurt.

Victor *and* **Rufus** *are back.*

Victor I might do what my great granddad did only discos not ballrooms.

Rufus Where will you get all your money from?

Victor Dancing. People pay you for dancing, you know, especially if you're famous. We could all be famous after today.

Billy *stumbles.* **Bernard** *picks him up.*

Bernard You OK? Come on, mate, come on.

Holds him up as they run.

Hannah Come on, Billy.

Janet
Lyndsay } Come on, Billy! Come on, Bernard!

Hannah *puts up 'Lap 14'.*

Victor How long, now?

Rufus You've been doing one hour and twenty minutes.

Janet *and* **Lyndsay** *come into the hall.*

Janet Hello, Victor. How are you doing?

Rufus Will you sign in, please?

Lyndsay Victor! Let me dance with you.

Janet We've had to come in for some more cakes. They're selling like hot cakes.

Lyndsay (*giving* **Victor** *a cake*) How are you doing?

Victor I'm all right. How are Billy and Bernard doing?

Lyndsay Fourteen laps. Hannah was telling me that Bernard's worked out he's getting about five pounds a lap.

Victor Mr Tong worked mine out. I'm getting about a pound every five minutes.

Rufus And some people have put money in the donations box.

Victor How much have you made?

Lyndsay Two pounds and five pence. Janet's only made one pound sixty cos she keeps eating all hers.

Janet Lyndsay, will you stop keep saying that. I've only had a few. Let me dance with him, I might get slim.

Lyndsay (*to* **Rufus**) How many necklaces have you sold?

Rufus Seven.

Lyndsay Don't forget me and Janet want one. Save us one, won't you?

Rufus I will.

Lyndsay They're really nice, Rufus. You're clever, aren't you?

Billy *stops, clutching his side.*

Billy I can't do any more.

Bernard *stops.*

Go on, don't stop.

Bernard Come on, just to the line.

Billy I'm having a rest. I'll see you next lap.

He sits. **Bernard** *runs on.* **Hannah** *gives him a drink.*

Hannah Is he all right?

Bernard Stitch.

Hannah Here. (*She gives him a note.*)

Bernard What's this?

Hannah Read it. (*She takes back the cup.*)

Hannah *stops.* **Bernard** *runs on. Reads.*

Hannah (*as* **Bernard** *reads*) I love you very much and I am very proud of you. Your Hannah.

Bernard *puts the note away somewhere.* **Hannah** *puts up 'Lap 18'.*

Loud Hailer Girls First Year high jump to Mrs Anderson by the fence. Will Carol Adams go to the parents enclosure, please? Your mum has brought your plimsolls.

Janet (*to* **Victor**) We'd better get back. See you later.

Lyndsay *and* **Janet** *go off.*

Rufus I'm off to see Bernard and Billy finish.

Victor You can't. You can't leave me. You've got to make sure I don't cheat. It won't be official.

Rufus You won't cheat. I won't be long.

Victor Get somebody to come in and watch me, then.

Rufus They'll all be watching the marathon.

Victor What's this, then? I've been dancing two hours!

Rufus Only another six to go!

Rufus *runs off.*

Loud Hailer Come on, then, give them a cheer. These boys are very tired. Here they come.

Bell rings. **Hannah** *puts up 'Lap 22'.*

Last lap now, come on, lads. They've been running for two hours.

Victor What about me?! Who's watching me?

Bernard *and* **Billy** *are cheered round.* **Hannah** *holds one end of the tape.* **Billy** *stumbles again.* **Bernard** *stops to pick him up. They go a bit further, urged on by the crowd.* **Billy** *stops again.* **Bernard** *picks him up, puts him on his back and they stagger to the line.* **Billy** *lets go and falls to the floor,* **Bernard** *falls into the arms of* **Hannah**. *Cheers.*

Loud Hailer Well done, boys, well done.

Victor *is wild as he hears the news, leaping, cheering and dancing about.* **Rufus, Hannah, Janet** *and* **Lyndsay** *take off* **Billy** *and* **Bernard**. **Victor** *is chanting 'Bernard! Bernard! Billy! Billy!' and clapping.*

Evening. School Hall

Janet *is setting up as DJ.* **Lyndsay** *is helping her. Music playing.*

Lyndsay Their Darrell says if I come along some night to their band rehearsal, they'll let me sing and see if I am any good for the band. They might let me do a couple of songs at their next gig.

Janet What's that?

Lyndsay Gig? Where the band plays. It's a musicians' word.

Janet You were coming round to our house tomorrow. My Dad was getting us 'Death Wish Three' from his video club.

Lyndsay I can't miss this chance. I might be famous.

Janet Yeah. (*Through microphone.*) Calling Mr Victor Gilbey. If Mr Victor Gilbey is in the building can he come to the main hall, please, as Yorkshire Television would like to interview him.

A mad scramble. **Victor** *and* **Rufus** *run on.*

Lyndsay They're not here, really.

Victor I was on the toilet.

Janet They must be enjoying themselves in Cleethorpes.

Lyndsay Yeah, on the fun fair.

Victor They were coming, honest. You ask Mr Tong.

Pause. **Victor** *dances on, very tired.*

Where's Bernard? I want him here to see me.

Lyndsay Hannah said he was going out collecting his sponsor money first.

Rufus We've got a new name for him, haven't we, Victor?

Victor Yes. St Bernard. (*Pause.*) Because he never gives in. Because he keeps going, and he helps other people. Like them dogs.

Janet St Bruno dogs.

Lyndsay Hey, we'll call him St Bernard when he comes in.

Janet Our Trixie went with one of them.

Victor *stumbles.* **Lyndsay** *pulls him up.*

Victor I wish St Bernard was here.

Janet How many do you think will be coming tonight?

Rufus I hope it gets full.

Lyndsay It's funny when it's empty, isn't it?

Janet How do you mean?

Lyndsay It just seems funny at night when you're in school and there's nobody about.

Janet Scary.

Lyndsay Spooky.

Janet *makes spooky noises through the microphone.*

Rufus I don't think that's funny.

Janet There's a ghost caretaker at this school, in't there, Lyndsay?

Lyndsay Yeah.

Janet They found his body one morning when they came in for assembly, hanging from them spotlights.

Lyndsay Turn all the lights off and see if he comes. (*She goes off.*)

Rufus No!

Janet Why not?

Rufus I won't be able to see if he's dancing.

Blackout. Spooky noises, screams, scuffles.

Put the lights on! Put the lights on!

The **Young Woman**'s *Flat*

Young Woman I can't pay you yet.

Bernard It's all right. I haven't come for the money. I just came to tell you I'd done it.

Young Woman I knew you would. I'm sorry, I forgot to watch the news.

Bernard We weren't on.

Young Woman Oh.

Bernard I think the murder must have took longer than they thought it would.

Young Woman How much are you going to get for doing it?

Bernard A hundred and twenty pounds fifteen pence if everybody pays up. I'm going to make sure that they do because some people might try and get out of it even though they've promised me the money. You get people who can't keep promises.

Young Woman I'll keep mine. Next Thursday I'll pay you, is that all right?

Bernard Doesn't he give you any money?

Young Woman Sometimes.

Bernard I would if I had a girlfriend who had had my baby. I'd work hard and get a good job so they could buy nice things. And I wouldn't let her live in a place like this, either.

Young Woman Where would you live?

Bernard Sheffield. I used to live in Sheffield. There's big houses and shops and only a bus ride away is the moors. Peak District.

Young Woman I went to Bakewell once.

Bernard When?!

Young Woman I went with school.

Bernard You might have seen me! I've been there loads of times.

Young Woman There was a river full of black fish.

Bernard Trout.

Young Woman We sat on the bank for our tea.

Bernard It's not changed. It's still the same.

Young Woman It was lovely.

Bernard You'll have to try and get there again. (*Pause.*) I'm going to have to go. Will you be all right?

Young Woman Yes. Somebody gave me some magazines to read this morning.

Bernard I might see you before Thursday – if you don't mind. Not for the money. Just to talk. I like talking to you. I seem to get on with older people.

They go off.

Wendy's *House*

Hannah *is gingerly helping* **Wendy** *on with her coat.*

Hannah Bernard's out collecting his money. You should have seen him today, Wendy. I think it was this afternoon that I realised I'm really and truly in love with him. (*Pause.*) Everybody's looking forward to seeing you. There's going to be loads there.

Billy's *House*

Billy Come on!

Linda Wait, will you?

Wendy's *House*

Wendy I won't have to say anything in front of all those people, will I?

Hannah No, we won't make you do that. Ready? Let's go and see if your mum's ready.

They go off.

Billy's *House*

Billy I'm going, I'll see you there.

Linda Sit down and wait!

Billy *shoots off.* **Linda** *gets up and follows.*

Corridor outside the Hall

Rufus *has a signing-in desk and donations tub outside the hall.*
We can hear music from inside and the occasional intro from **Janet**
on the mike. **Hannah** *comes out.*

Hannah Hello, Rufus.

Rufus Hello, Hannah. Look at all these people.

Shows her the book.

Hello, Miss.

Hannah Hello, Miss.

Rufus Can you sign the book, Miss?

Hannah Yes, Miss, he's still dancing. Isn't he, Rufus?

Rufus He hasn't stopped, Miss, honest. Yes, Miss he's
tired out. Isn't he?

Hannah Yes, Miss. I don't know if he's going to last till
eight o'clock. Enjoy yourself, Miss.

Rufus (*to* **Hannah**) Look who's come. (*Shows book.*)

Hannah Who?

Rufus My cousin Jane and my Aunty Maureen. They
bought a necklace and a bracelet.

Darrell *appears.*

Darrell Hi. Many in?

Hannah Darrell. (*She takes him aside.*) Will you stop telling
Lyndsay all these lies about your band?

Darrell What you on about?

Hannah You know. She's going round telling everybody
she might be singing in a famous band.

Darrell We might be famous. Everybody's got to start somewhere. We might let her join. You're just jealous.

Hannah I know you. It's all dreams.

Darrell It's not dreams, then, we're gonna do it. We've got a gig. What's it got to do with you?

Hannah She's my friend.

Darrell She might be mine after tonight.

He makes to go in.

Hannah Darrell. Please. Don't treat her like a fool, like everybody else does. She's got feelings. She's only sixteen.

He goes in.

Wendy *comes out.*

Wendy Where's Lyndsay?

Hannah In the toilet putting her costume on.

Wendy Where's Bernard?

Hannah I don't know.

Rufus Yes, Miss? What's wrong? A phone call for me? (*To* **Hannah**.) Will you look after my table for me?

Hannah Yes, we'll be here.

Rufus *goes off.*

Hannah This was going to be the best night of my life.

Wendy He'll be here. You get worried when you're in love.

Hannah Do you? I must be, then, eh?

Wendy Yes.

They see **Lyndsay** *approaching.* **Hannah** *nudges* **Wendy**.

Lyndsay Hiya.

Hannah Will you sign in please?

Lyndsay It's me!

Hannah Sorry?

Lyndsay Lyndsay. Oh, you!

They laugh.

Hannah You look fantastic.

Lyndsay Do I?

Hannah Doesn't she?

Wendy Yes. You look lovely.

Lyndsay I'm nervous. Feel.

They hold hands.

Hannah Your big night.

Lyndsay Oooh. (*Pause.*) We'll remember this, won't we?

Hannah I'll always remember it.

Lyndsay Even after you've married Bernard?

Hannah I'll tell my grandchildren about it.

Lyndsay If I have a little girl I'm going to call her Hannah.

Wendy If I have any, I'll call my first Hannah and my second Lyndsay.

Lyndsay I can't think of us as mums, being old.

Wendy I don't want to get old.

Hannah Stay sixteen for ever.

Lyndsay My mum says she still feels sixteen in her head, but she can't do. I mean, she never has a laugh or anything.

Hannah They have too many things to worry about.

Bernard *arrives.*

Bernard! (*Rushes to him and flings herself in his arms.*)

Bernard I got made late.

Hannah I've been worried about you.

Lyndsay *and* **Wendy** *go in.*

Bernard I've been getting some of my money. Some of the old women kept me talking, asking me all about it.

Hannah Victor's been asking for you all night.

Bernard How is he?

Rufus *rushes in.*

Hannah He'll feel better if you talk to him. You can keep him going.

Rufus I've got a brother! I've got a little brother. My mam's had him tonight! I'm a brother!

Hannah Oh, Rufus. (*Hugs him.*)

Bernard That's great.

Rufus *dashes inside.* **Bernard** *signs in. A record finishes.* **Janet** *introduces* **Lyndsay** *as Madonna. We hear the record begin.* **Bernard** *and* **Hannah** *go in.*

The School Hall

Lyndsay *is singing and dancing to Madonna.* **Victor** *is staggering. He sees* **Bernard** *as do all the others. A cheer and a clap for him. He clasps* **Victor** *as a close friend, dances with him, keeps him going through the song.* **Lyndsay** *finishes. Claps. A new record begins.*

Janet (*stopping record*) Excuse me. Can I have your attention, please? I've got a special announcement. Rufus has got a little brother. (*Cheers.*) Right. Now, it's nearly eight o'clock and Victor is coming up to finishing his eight hour non-stop dancing marathon. (*Cheers.*) Synchronise watches. One minute to go. (*Clapping.*) Come on, Victor!

Wendy *steps up to the microphone.*

Wendy Ten, nine . . .

Everyone joins in.

All Zero!

Cheers, clapping, etc. **Victor** *is put on* **Bernard**'*s shoulders and paraded round the hall. The action gradually changes to slow motion and we see* **Victor**, *beaming. Mixed with the music we hear* **Victor**'*s prayer.*

Victor Thank you, Lord. Thank you for watching over us and making it the happiest night of my life. I think that we will be able to buy the microwave and some books for the library if everyone pays up. Mrs Anderson said we could put our names in the books so that after we've left next week other boys and girls will see where they came from.

Wendy and her mum went home very happy. I don't mean because of all the money – I think her mum saw how much we are all very close to each other. I think we will stay friends for always after tonight, don't you? By the way, any day now I think Bernard might ask me to be his best man. I hope he does.

Thank you for Rufus's baby brother. He wants his mum to call him Bernard.

Geography Lesson

They settle down to begin work.

Hannah Miss, I don't know why he's away again today. I haven't seen him since Saturday.

Janet I bet.

Hannah I haven't. Everybody keeps asking me and I don't know.

Janet You're his girlfriend. You go round to his house.

Hannah No I don't.

Lyndsay Haven't you been to their house? Why not? (*Pause.*) I'm only asking her, Miss. Sorry, Hannah.

Janet It's none of her business, is it, Miss?

Victor It might be tonsiliters because he was singing a lot on Friday night, wasn't he? He might have lost his voice.

Billy I bet he's getting all the money in.

Victor Miss! I know where his voice is. It must be in the hall. The caretaker might have swept it up!

Rufus *gives out work sheets.*

Miss, we've done this one. We have, haven't we?

Janet What is it?

Victor The word search on towns.

Janet No.

Victor We have, because I remember Bernard found Sheffield for me.

Janet Oh, yeah.

Lyndsay We have, Miss, we've done this one.

Rufus *collects them up again. Gives out a new lot.*

Victor What's this one? Rivers. We've got rivers this time.

Billy *comes forward.*

Billy's *Careers Interview*

Billy (*reading*) William Starkey, 22 Brasenby House.

Mother – forecourt attendant, petrol station.

Sister – hairdresser.

My career ideas – jockey, farmer, painter and decorator, cook.

(*Looking up.*) I wanted to be a policeman, Miss, but I don't think I'll grow that far up.

(*Reading.*) My work experience – I worked at Levitt Halt riding stables.

(*Looking up.*) Mucking out, mainly, brushing the horses and cleaning the tack. Brilliant, Miss. No, Miss, I was too busy to do any riding. No, Miss, I haven't ridden a horse yet.

(*Reading.*) Courses – RAF talk. Tech college talk.

(*Looking up.*) I thought about cookery. I wouldn't mind being a chef in a pub.

(*Reading.*) Personal likes – horses, American football, police films, war films.

Geography Lesson

Victor Awk. Pretty Polly.

Lyndsay I've finished.

Janet You haven't got the Humber.

Lyndsay You shouldn't be looking.

Lyndsay Humber isn't on, anyway.

Janet It is. I've got it. I've got more than you.

Lyndsay Where?

Billy Don't show her. You've got to do it on your own. Miss!

Victor Pretty Polly. Miss, River Parrott. River Parrott, Miss. Awk. Do you get it? (*Pause.*) Four, Miss.

Billy Six, Miss.

Janet Eleven, Miss.

Wendy Five, Miss.

Hannah Two, Miss.

The others laugh, pack away. All go except **Rufus**, *tidying up, and* **Hannah**. *She comes forward.*

Hannah Miss, I am worried about him. It's not like Bernard to be poorly. He must be really bad. I don't go to their house because Bernard told me not to. He said his dad's a bit funny about people coming to the house. But I will tonight, Miss, I don't care. I've got to see him. Yes, Miss, I will. Goodnight. (*She goes.*)

Rufus Miss, my mum told me to tell you thank you very much for the nice card and the flowers. (*Gets out a small card. Reads.*) Robert Howard Croft, born 7.40 pm, Friday,

July 10th 1991. Weight, 7lb 4oz. Eyes blue, hair dark brown. (*Puts card away.*) Goodnight, Miss.

Rufus *goes.*

A Row of Houses

Victor *is at one door,* **Billy** *the next.* **Victor** *knocks,* **Billy** *knocks. While they are waiting they pull faces at each other.* **Victor** *is pulling a particularly grotesque face when his door is opened.*

Victor Oh, er, I've come to tell you I've done my dance marathon. You owe me eighty p. (*Shows form.*) Thank you.

They pull faces again.

Billy I've brought my form. (*Hands it over.*) Forty-four pence.

Victor Thank you very much indeed. Goodnight.

Victor *puts the money in a handbag. He fits a bike lock through the handles and fastens it round his neck.*

Billy Thanks. (*Takes money. To* **Victor**.) What are you doing?

Victor If I get mugged, they can't take my money.

They go off.

A Department Store

Janet Excuse me. I want a bottle of Charlie eau de toilette spray perfume, please. It's a leaving present for one of our teachers. We're leaving on Friday. And have you got any nice thank-you cards? I want one with dogs on. I'm sorry but it's all in two pences and ten pences.

Voice You're on the wrong counter love. Over that side.

Janet Oh. (*Moving off.*) Excuse me, have you got Charlie?

Bernard's *House*

Hannah *knocks at the door.*

Hannah Hello. Is your Bernard in?

Voice He's not living here any more.

Hannah Is this Bernard Easley's house?

Voice He's in Sheffield. Thinks he's a man now. Got hisself another family.

Hannah *moves off.*

Bernard's *Dad's voice* Is she from school? Eh! I don't want anybody here after no sponsor money. It's got nowt to do with us.

Hannah's *House*

Darrell What's up?

Lyndsay I'm scared.

Darrell You'll be all right.

Lyndsay There's only tonight and that's it.

Darrell How many rehearsals do you need for one number?

Lyndsay I haven't even met the rest of the band yet.

Darrell You'll be all right. You've learnt it anyway.

Lyndsay It's not the same, learning it off your tape. They might not like me.

Darrell I said we'd be there at eight.

Lyndsay What have you told them about me?

Darrell I said you're good.

Lyndsay You didn't. What did you say that for? What did they say?

Darrell They'll see for themselves.

Lyndsay Oh no.

Darrell If you're like this meeting the band, what are you going to be like tomorrow?

Lyndsay Will there be many there?

Darrell We didn't have time to do any posters, cos like we were still thinking up a name, but everybody knows we're on. Loads of our mates are off.

Hannah *enters. Sits.*

Lyndsay Hannah. What's wrong?

Darrell Are you all right? She's been a bit funny about leaving school.

Lyndsay What's happened? Is it Bernard? Is he real poorly?

Darrell What's up?

Pause.

Darrell We've got to go. You going to be all right?

Lyndsay He'll be all right, Hannah. He's strong. He'll get better. Don't worry. He'll get better. (*Pause.*) Wish me luck with the band.

Hannah Good luck, Lyndsay.

Darrell See you later.

Darrell *and* **Lyndsay** *go.* **Hannah** *begins to sob.*

Hannah Please, God, make him come back. Please. Don't let me lose him. I don't want to be without Bernard. Please.

A Street

Victor *and* **Billy** *enter.* **Victor** *has forgotten the bike lock combination.*

Victor Try another number!

Billy I'm fed up with trying. You'll have to get your dad to saw it off. Or the fire brigade.

Victor My dad'll hit me.

Another Street

Rufus *comes to a bus stop where a lady is stood. He has a bunch of flowers.*

Rufus Excuse me. Is this the stop for the hospital bus?

Pause. **Rufus** *gets out his little card and begins reading it out to the lady, proud.*

Robert Howard Croft . . .

Wendy's *House*

Wendy *is finishing off a long banner on which we can see written* 'Goodbye Miss and good luck. Love from Class Five'.

The Playground, next day

Wendy *is comforting* **Hannah**. *The others are close by.* **Victor** *is muttering to himself and shaking his head.*

Janet I'm off to kill him, he's a bastard.

Wendy Don't Janet, you're making it worse.

Janet Well he is. He can't have really loved you to do that.

Billy Nearly ninety quid he must have gone off with. We can't even get the microwave now.

Janet Who's this girl he's gone off with? Some slag I bet.

Victor Can't we go to Sheffield and bring him back?

Janet When did they go?

Lyndsay Sunday.

Victor (*to* **Hannah**) We still love you, anyway. Don't forget that. Don't we?

Lyndsay Yes. I'm sorry, Hannah, I had to tell them. They had to know because of the money.

Janet If he ever comes back here he's dead. Not cos of the money, cos of what it's done to Hannah.

Billy What about the money, though? Where do we get it from now?

Wendy My mum won't mind. It doesn't matter.

Victor I can't believe it. Maybe we've got it all wrong. He was Saint Bernard, wasn't he?

Rufus We couldn't have done any of it without him.

Maths Lesson

Lyndsay Sorry we're late, Miss, we were having a meeting and we didn't know the bell had gone.

Janet Miss, we're not doing any work are we? We're leaving on Friday.

Lyndsay Can we just read, Miss? I don't think anybody wants to play any games. Do we?

Janet No, Miss.

Victor No, Miss.

Billy Miss, can me and Victor do some sums?

Victor Eh? What do you want to say that for? Miss, don't take any notice. He doesn't feel very well.

Billy I want to work out what money we've got.

Victor We've done it all.

Billy I need to know how much short we are now, cos of Bernard.

Janet Shurrup!

Lyndsay Don't say anything. (*Pause.*) Hannah? Shall I tell her?

Billy Somebody's got to.

Lyndsay Miss, can I just have a word with Hannah a minute?

Lyndsay *goes to* **Hannah**, *whispers.*

Victor It's about Bernard, Miss.

Janet *swipes at him.*

Janet I've told you.

Hannah *gets up.*

Wendy Miss, can I take Hannah to the toilet?

Hannah *and* **Wendy** *go out.*

Lyndsay (*coming to the front*) Bernard's left, Miss. He's not coming back. He's gone to Sheffield with the sponsor money he's collected.

She gets upset and rushes out.

Janet Miss, can I go and see if she's all right? Thanks, Miss.

Janet *goes out.*

Rufus Where are the girls going?

Victor They're having a lesson in the toilet.

Rufus Oh. Miss, can I do a word search? (*Gets one.*)

Billy Miss, can I go and borrow a calculator off Mr Tong? (*Goes.*)

Victor *is bored.*

Victor Miss, do you believe in sex before marriage? Sorry, Miss. (*Pause.*) Bernard's gone off with a woman. (*Pause.*) I do know, Miss. Hannah said his mum told her. (*Pause. To* **Rufus**.) He might get aids. (*Pause.*) Miss, will they send the twag man for him? Why not? Could we not bother coming to school this week, then? Wouldn't they bother sending the twag man for us? (*Pause.*) I'm off. (*Gets up.*) See you. (*Starts to walk out.*) Miss, I'm not really.

Wendy *enters.*

Wendy Miss, Janet and Lyndsay are looking after Hannah. She won't come back up. (*Pause.*) All right, Miss.

Wendy's *Careers Interview*

Wendy Wendy Lobley, 57 Wilder Street. (*Looks up.*) I've not filled any more in, Miss, with my being away. (*Pause.*) They give me these pills but they make me slow. A man at the hospital talked to me about what I'm going to be able to do. I can't do factory work with machines, I can't do any job where it might be dangerous to other people if I have a fit. I can't drive a car. That's all, Miss. It all depends on whether I get better or worse. (*Pause.*) I'm allowed to work in a shop. I'm allowed to do office work. I'm allowed to get married and have babies.

Billy *rushes in. Stops suddenly.*

Billy Oh. Miss, can Wendy go out a minute?

Wendy What for?

Billy Private.

Wendy I'll see how they are, Miss.

Billy You don't have to go, Miss. (*Pause.*) Do you trust us?

Victor We will be sensible.

Wendy (*to teacher as they go out*) I'm going to be sad tomorrow, Miss. I know I'm hardly ever here, but when I am I love it here. I've been happy here.

Wendy *goes.*

Billy Listen, we're only fifteen quid short of a microwave.

Victor Oh. That's it, then.

Billy Are you just going to let it all go after what we've done? Fifteen quid? We can get that, can't we?

Victor How?

Billy We can't just give up because of Bernard.

Victor No. No, you're right. Why should we let him stop us? (*Pause.*) We've only got tonight.

Billy Mr Tong said he'd get it for us tomorrow dinner if we had the rest of the money in the morning.

Victor Nobody will want to give me any more money.

Billy Think of something. Rufus!

Rufus What?

Billy Think of something.

They think.

Rufus I think the bell's gone.

They go.

Home Time

The girls bring **Hannah** *into the playground.*

Victor Is she all right?

Lyndsay I think so. Will you be all right?

Hannah Yes, thanks.

Victor I'm sorry it's upset you.

Wendy Are you sure you want to go home on your own?

Hannah Yes. Goodbye.

Lyndsay Hannah. You've still got us. Mates.

All watch her go, saying their goodbyes.

Janet We'll all be coming out of school for the last time, tomorrow, won't we?

Wendy Bye.

She goes off. They say their goodbyes to her.

Billy We've got to make fifteen quid tonight. That's all we need for a microwave. What can we do? (*Pause.*) Come on, what?

Lyndsay I can't. I'm singing tonight. I've got my first gig.

Janet Oh yes, I forgot. Best of luck, Lyndsay.

Lyndsay Thanks.

Janet I'd come and watch you but –

Lyndsay No. Honest, Janet, I don't want anybody seeing me.

Janet I can't anyway. I've got to go with my dad to take Trixie to the vets for a hysterectomy.

Billy Oh, thanks. That's good, in't it? After all we've done.

Victor Yes, thanks.

Lyndsay I'm sorry. I don't even want to do this singing now. I don't feel in the mood. But I can't let them down.

Victor Me and you, then.

Billy Yes.

They move off, saying their goodbyes.

I'll be round after my tea. Get thinking.

Lyndsay *looks up at the school.*

Janet What's wrong?

Lyndsay I'm going to miss the place.

Janet Lyndsay?

Lyndsay Everything's going to be all right, isn't it, Janet?

Janet What about? Tonight?

Lyndsay About everything. I don't want things to change. It will all be memories after tomorrow, won't it?

They go off.

On the Way Home

Hannah *enters.*

Girl's Voice Hey, Hannah! Hey, Hannah!

Hannah *stops.*

Where's your boyfriend tonight? She's getting married to him, aren't you?

Girl's Voice 2 Leave her.

Girl's Voice 1 What?

Girl's Voice 2 Leave her. (*To* **Hannah**.) Don't take any notice of her. (*To* **Girl 1**.) You shouldn't pick on funny people. She can't help being like that.

Hannah *moves off.*

Girl's Voice 1 (*to* **Girl 2**) Just cos you fancy her brother.

Victor's *House*

Victor Just when everything seems to be going right it all starts to go wrong again, doesn't it? Why does it do that? Is it you that makes it happen? Is it because we've all got a bit too pleased with ourselves for what we've done? Did you think we thought we'd done it all ourselves without your help? Is that why you've changed everything?

I'm sorry. I did start to think I was a bit good. And when everyone cheered me at the end I thought I was great. Was that so wrong of me? Is that why you've sent Bernard to Sheffield and hurt Hannah? Because of me? Because you know how much I care about them both? Please, God, hurt me, don't hurt Hannah. Don't make her feel bad. She never has a nasty thought in her life.

Janet's *voice* Will you make sure that our Trixie is all right after her operation? Don't let her die in the middle of it, will you?

Rufus's *voice* Will you make sure my mum still keeps loving me now she's got Robert? I'm going home tomorrow. Thank you for making my Aunty Maureen not say anything to me about the wet bed.

Wendy's *voice* Do you think if I get a bit better someone might marry me? I can have my babies, then, can't I?

Hannah's *voice* When I prayed for my dad to come back, he didn't, did he? So why should I ask you for Bernard?

Lyndsay's *voice* I want tonight to go fast because I'm nervous and I want tomorrow to go slow because it's our last day.

Billy *appears by* **Victor**.

Billy Your mam sent me up.

Victor Oh.

Billy (*tapping a roll of material under his arm*) I've got the answer to all our prayers.

Victor What's that?

Billy A magic carpet. Come on.

They go.

Hannah*'s House*

Wendy, Hannah *and* **Lyndsay** *are waiting.* **Darrell** *can be heard on the phone. The call finishes, he enters.*

Darrell That was Pete. He says he's got his dad's van.

Lyndsay Oh, good.

Darrell Yeah, but he's taking all the gear and he won't be able to come back to pick us up because there isn't enough petrol so we have to go on the bus.

They begin to collect up several plastic bags of gear.

Lyndsay (*to* **Hannah** *and* **Wendy**) See you.

They say their goodbyes. **Darrell** *and* **Lyndsay** *leave.*

Wendy Do you want to come round to my house?

Hannah I don't think so.

Wendy Come on. I'll show you the card I've done for Miss. My mum got me a film for my camera today. And an autograph book.

Hannah I don't want to see your mum.

Wendy I've told you, she's not bothered about it. She's

upset for all you lot after what you've done, not for herself. Please come round with me.

They go.

Outside a Pub

Billy *and* **Victor** *arrive.* **Billy** *rolls out a dancing mat. They both put on dark glasses and woolly hats.* **Billy** *sets up a sign. It reads:*

'All money to St Peter's Special School to buy urgent equitment. Totley blind. Please give a lot.'

They switch on a tape recorder and begin to dance. **Billy** *does robotics and break-dancing.* **Victor** *tries to copy.*

Voice Oi! Get out of it. Go on, clear off!

They start to collect things up, pretending to be blind.

Go on, move! Who said you could set up outside my pub? Did you ask? Eh? Did you hell. Hop it!

Another Pub. Ladies Toilet

A woman knocks on one of the doors.

Woman's *voice* Hello? Are you all right, love? They want you on stage.

Lyndsay No.

Voice They're waiting. What's wrong?

Lyndsay I can't do the singing.

Darrell's *voice* Where is she?

Voice Hey, get out! You can't come in the ladies!

Banging on the door.

Darrell's *voice* Hey! Get out here!

Lyndsay No, I can't. Just leave me alone. I'm not going on.

Darrell's *voice* Don't sod about, come on!

Lyndsay I can't, Darrell, I can't.

If I go out there, I won't sing. I mean it. Do something else – go on – do another song.

I know what you think of me. I'm sorry. I can't remember the song. I can't remember it. I'm scared. I'm sorry. I feel sick.

Darrell's *voice* Me too. Thanks. Thanks a lot.

A Street

Victor *and* **Billy** *appear.*

Billy This pub'll do.

Starts to set up.

Victor I'm just going to the public conveniences. I won't be long.

Goes off, leaving **Billy** *to set up.*

Wendy*'s House*

Wendy *is showing* **Hannah** *a photo album.*

Wendy These are all when we went to York. There's
Bernard, look, right up at the top. Look at Victor!

Hannah What is he doing?

Wendy Don't you remember they hung him over the side
and pretended they were going to let go? There's you and
me.

Hannah Janet's eating again.

They flip through more pages.

Janet*'s House*

Janet *is sorting out presents and cards.*

Janet Right. Mr Tong, Mrs Edminds, Mrs Wilkinson,
Miss Bennett, Mr Oliver the headmaster, Mr Caretaker
man.

(*Picks up two presents.*) I'd better not give Mrs Anderson
Trixie's get-well present. Which is which? (*Sniffs.*) Charlie.
Good Boy Choc Drops.

She writes some more cards.

Ladies Toilets in Pub

Woman's *voice* (*tapping*) Are you still there, love?

Lyndsay Yes.

Woman's *voice* I think you'd better go before they finish. They're not very pleased with you.

A Street

Victor *returns to* **Billy**.

Victor This man says he might be able to get me fifteen pounds!

Billy Eh? How?

Victor He might be able to get me some money later on if I go now.

Billy Where?

Victor I don't know. Just for a walk.

Billy Come on, then.

Victor No. Just me.

Billy Who is he?

Victor I've seen him before. I don't know his name. He stops and talks to me sometimes. Fifteen quid! I told him what we'd been doing and he thought it was great and he said he'd like to help us. I think he's just a bit lonely and he wants to give us the money so I'll be his friend. I'll see you later.

Billy What about me?

Victor You're already my friend.

Billy Aren't we doing this, now?

Victor (*running off*) I'll see you tomorrow.

Billy *is left to pack up on his own.*

Ladies Toilet, Pub

Banging on door.

Voice 1 Hey! Get out here!

Voice 2 Come on!

Darrell's *voice* Leave her.

Voice 1 No chuffing way. She's not doing that to me and getting away with it.

Voice 2 She's out. She's well out.

Voice 1 Come on!

More banging on the door.

Lyndsay Darrell!

Darrell's *voice* What are you going to do to her?

Voice 1 You start packing the stuff in the van.

Lyndsay Darrell!

Voice 2 (*quieter now*) He's gone. Are you coming out or are we coming in?

Lyndsay I want to go home.

Voice 1 We're not going home yet. We're off for a drive. Come on, we're off to celebrate our success.

Voice 2 (*quiet*) Few drinks. Back of the van. You can be my groupie, if you like. Come on. We'll make sure you get home.

Pause, then furious banging on the door and yelling.

Last Day of Term. On the Way to School

Hannah *is with* **Lyndsay**.

Hannah I won't tell anybody. (*Pause.*) You just left and came home on your own?

Lyndsay Yes. Yes, I walked home. Is that what Darrell told you?

Hannah Yes. Why?

Lyndsay Nothing.

She begins to get upset.

Hannah Lyndsay?

Janet *arrives.*

Janet Hiya! What's up? I know, it's awful, isn't it? I've been upset. Packing my school bag for the last time. How did it go last night? Was it good?

Lyndsay Not really.

Janet Why, what happened?

Hannah She says she wasn't very good but I bet she was.

Janet Yeah. I bet you were really good. Was you nervous?

Lyndsay Yes.

Janet That's nothing. Everybody is when they first do it.

They move on towards school.

Billy *arrives with* **Victor**.

Victor My dad gave me the money!

Billy Puff.

Victor Don't say that, it's not true! Don't keep saying it, Billy, don't tell people that. I never. I never, honest!

Billy Puff puff. (*Begins to do a puffing train around him.*)

Victor Billy! I'm not. I went for a walk but he started to make me feel scared so I left him. I did! I swear my dad gave me the money.

Billy I bet.

Victor OK, I bet you. Ask him tonight. You've got to believe me!

Billy *puffs off.*

Don't say anything, please!

Wendy *enters with her camera at the ready.*

Wendy Victor! (*He looks up.*) Smile, please.

She takes a shot of him.

You're supposed to get upset when we leave this afternoon, not when we're going in this morning. (*Links arms.*) Come on.

They move off.

A Classroom

Janet Miss, come on, come and have your photo taken.

Rufus In the middle, Miss.

Billy On my knee, Miss.

Janet *takes a group photo.*

Wendy Miss, have you signed my autograph book yet?

Janet And mine. Come on, Miss, you're taking a long time to think what to put. Just put 'Best Wishes to my favourite pupil'.

Wendy Miss, can I go and see Mr Tong?

Janet She wants to give him a kiss.

Wendy No.

Janet She wants to tell him she loves him before she goes.

Billy Mr Tong?

Janet Shurrup, he's brilliant. He's all cuddly. Can I go as well, Miss?

Wendy I've got a present for him, Miss. Thanks. (*Goes.*)

Billy Hey, Miss, we've got the money for the microwave.

Cheers.

Janet How did you get it?

Victor Have you got a Bible, Miss? I need one. (*Runs off.*)

Billy He got fifteen quid.

Janet Where from?

Billy I'm not telling.

Janet Miss, we're not taking it if he's nicked it.

Billy Somebody gave him it.

Janet Who?

Victor *returns with Bible.*

Billy (*quietly*) Puff puff puff . . .

Victor I swear that the evidence I shall give shall be the truth, the whole truth and nothing but the truth, so help me God. LISTEN TO ME! My dad gave me all this money. (*Pushes it on* **Hannah**.) My dad gave it me.

Billy Miss, can I have a word with Victor a minute? (*Goes to him.*) I'm sorry, Victor. I've not said anything, honest. Have I?

Janet What about? What's up with him?

Hannah Victor? Don't, Victor.

Lyndsay Sit with us.

They hold hands. He sits between **Lyndsay** *and* **Hannah**.

Janet Miss, I bet he nicked it.

Billy Shut it!

Lyndsay Leave it, Janet.

Janet What? Oh, God, I won't speak to anybody if you like.

Billy Good. (*He sits down.*)

Rufus Miss, can we play that game? Where you do mimes? Yes. Give us a Clue, that's it. I've got one. I don't know how to do it. Hannah, come and do this with me.

Hannah *comes out and together they work their way through a mime for 'Puff the Magic Dragon' – nobody gets it.*

Janet Planet of the Apes.

Billy You're not speaking!

Janet Oh, God!

Billy Planet of the Apes.

Rufus No.

Wendy *enters.*

Wendy Bernard's back.

All ask 'Where?' etc. **Hannah**, *not hearing, is still doing her mime.* **Wendy** *goes to her, taps her.*

Bernard is on the school field.

The others go over to the window and look out.

Victor What has he got?

Billy Beer cans.

Lyndsay Is he drunk?

Janet Miss, look, Bernard's got some beer.

Billy I bet he bought it with the money.

Janet What does he want? Miss, can we go out? (*Pause.*) It's nearly playtime.

They all sit down.

(*To* **Hannah**.) Do you want me to smack him?

Lyndsay (*to* **Hannah**) Are you going to see him?

Hannah *shakes her head.*

Victor He might have brought us some of the money.

Hannah No, we don't want it.

Lyndsay Why isn't he coming in?

Billy He's scared to. He's scared of Miss.

All Bell's gone, Miss. (*Etc.*)

They all shoot out, except **Hannah** *and* **Rufus**. **Rufus** *comes out front.*

Rufus Can we finish off our mime after break, Miss? It was Puff the Magic Dragon. (*Disappointed.*) Oh.

He goes out after the others.

The School Field

Bernard *is clutching his cans. The others rush on and stop some way from him. No one dares go near. Pause.*

Bernard Why don't you just say you hate me?

Janet We hate you.

Bernard I've got some money left.

Janet Shove it.

Bernard Victor?

Billy You don't know what he's done to make up the money you took.

Victor *runs off.*

Lyndsay We don't need your money now. It's too late.

Billy We don't need you any more.

Janet What do you want? What have you come back for?

Wendy Hannah won't see you.

Lyndsay No, she won't.

Janet Can't blame her. She's got somebody else.

Lyndsay Who?

Janet You know.

Lyndsay No. Oh, yeah.

Janet She's going out with Victor.

Lyndsay Is she?

Wendy Don't tell him that. She isn't.

Billy He's a puff, anyway.

Bernard I just want to see her.

Lyndsay She won't.

Bernard I'll wait, then. I'll see her going home.

Lyndsay Wait, then.

Janet Yeah, wait, then. She won't see you. Come on.

They drift off.

Billy (*going up to him*) See you, you bloody thieving get!
(*Darts off, but* **Bernard** *makes no move.*)

Bernard Wendy!

Wendy *comes back.*

I know what I've done and I know what everybody thinks
and it makes me feel like jumping off the bridge onto the
motorway. Will you just tell her I . . . tell her . . .

Wendy I'll tell her.

She goes off. **Bernard** *slowly follows.*

The Classroom

Hannah *is comforting* **Victor**.

Hannah We all care about you. You'll always be special.

Victor But why is he saying them things? Billy shouldn't
say things like that about me. They're not true. I never did
anything to anybody. I only talk to people. That's all
right, isn't it?

Hannah You mustn't talk to strangers.

Victor I talk to God sometimes but I don't think he
listens. I don't think he cares about me.

Hannah I believe he listens.

Victor Do you?

Hannah Can you keep a secret?

Victor Cross my heart.

Hannah Don't say anything but I prayed for Bernard to come back. I still want him, Victor. Don't tell.

Lyndsay *enters.*

Lyndsay We've all got to go down to the hall now. It's our leaving assembly.

They go out.

The Hall

The group file in, sit on the floor. **Victor, Hannah** *and* **Lyndsay** *follow.*

Voice Let us pray.

They bow their heads.

Oh Lord, watch over us and grant that the friendships formed between us here may neither be broken nor forgotten but that bound together by thy love, we may draw nearer to thee and nearer to each other, through Jesus Christ our Lord. Amen.

They raise their heads, but another prayer follows.

We commend, Lord, unto thy care, our friends about to leave this school. We ask thee to keep them from temptation and danger. May thy loving kindness and mercy follow them all the days of their life. Amen.

They raise their heads, tearful now.

Victor *stands, gets out a tiny scrap of paper, reads*

Victor Three cheers for all the teachers! Hip hip!

All Hooray!

Victor *sits down.* **Lyndsay** *nudges him. He looks at the paper.*

Victor Hip hip!

All Hooray!

Victor Hip hip!

All Hooray!

Victor (*to* **Lyndsay**) How many's that?

They all stand.

Lyndsay (*to* **Hannah**) Are you sure you don't want to do it?

Hannah *shakes her head.*

(*To the staff, reading from a note.*) We just want to say thank you all for putting up with us. We're going to miss you. We're all very sorry that we couldn't get any books for the library, but we have got something to give Wendy and her mum. From all the school and all the people who gave us money . . .

Janet (*reading from a note*) A cheque to buy the microwave. From all the pupils and staff at St Peter's Special School and all your friends. (*Gives* **Wendy** *the cheque.*)

Billy (*reading from a note*) We didn't have time to get the microwave but this is how much one costs.

They clap her.

Wendy Thank you. We'll buy it tomorrow. Anybody who wants to come round and see it working in our kitchen, they can do.

A hymn is begun: 'In the name of Jesus . . .' The gang sing with gusto. During the second verse the scene begins to dissolve and we are back in:

The Classroom

More signing of autographs, photographs.

Billy I'll see you, then, Miss. (*Pause.*) I wouldn't mind starting all over again as a First Year. I'm small enough, aren't I? Do you think you could smuggle me in?

Hannah Miss, can I take Bernard's picture file?

She takes it. A few more goodbyes.

Janet Miss, we're all going to stay friends. I'm having a leaving party tomorrow at my house and everybody's coming. Do you want to come, Miss?

All Yes, go on, Miss. (*Etc.*)

Janet All right, Miss.

Victor We'll drink some toasts to you, anyway.

Hannah Can I go to the toilet, Miss? (*She goes.*)

Janet My mam is buying us two bottles of that Pomagne. You know, it's like champagne only cheaper.

A few more goodbyes. A photo grouping. **Victor** *takes the picture.*

Janet Come on, Victor! Press it!

They freeze.

The School Field

Hannah *goes over to* **Bernard**.

Hannah Hello, Bernard.

Bernard Hello, Hannah.

Hannah Are you drunk?

Bernard A bit.

Hannah Why?

Bernard Will you take me back?

Hannah I don't know.

Bernard I'm sorry for everything.

Hannah Are you back now?

Bernard Yes.

Hannah Good. I've missed you. I've got your picture file.

Gives it to him.

Will you wait for me? I won't be long.

Hannah *moves off.*

Bernard I'll wait at the gate.

The Classroom

Victor *takes the picture – flash.*

Victor Miss, I didn't get to do my careers interview, did I? It's all right, Miss, I think I might be getting a job at Henley's woodyard, where I was on work experience. It was great. They were a good laugh. They put some sawdust in one of my sandwiches and I ate it! I wondered what everybody was laughing at. I brought Mr Tong's gerbil a great big bag of shavings. They let me have it for nothing! (*Pause.*) I'll see you, then. I'll miss you, Miss. Hey, did you hear what I said? 'Miss you Miss'. That's funny, isn't it?

Hannah Goodbye, then, Miss. Thank you for being my teacher and for teaching me all about life. I'll try not to forget. I wish you happiness for ever.

Lyndsay, Janet, Wendy *and* **Hannah** *join hands and link up with* **Rufus** *and* **Billy**. *They hold up* **Wendy**'s *'Goodbye Miss and Good Luck' sign.*

Lyndsay Miss, we're going to walk backwards all the way out of the school till we get to the school gates so we don't turn our backs on the school.

They start to move off. **Billy** *holds on to* **Victor**'s *hand.*

All Goodbye, Miss.

They are gone.

Printed in the United Kingdom
by Lightning Source UK Ltd.
116998UKS00001B/53